We live in a world desperately in need of Spirit-baptized, Spirit-filled, and Spirit-empowered people. In his book *Gateway to a Supernatural Life*, Jeff Leake provides a Bible-saturated tour of the life every Christian should long for and experience. Read this book expecting your life to change!

—*John Lindell*
Lead Pastor, James River Church, Springfield, MO

Jeff has written another devotional book that has the potential to change your Christian walk dramatically. Get your hands on *Gateway to a Supernatural Life* and grow spiritually.

—*Rob Ketterling*
Lead Pastor, River Valley Church, Apple Valley, MN

I have met many world leaders, professional athletes, and successful businesspeople, yet Jeff Leake always stands out to me as one of the finest men I have been privileged to know. He doesn't encourage others to walk where he has not walked himself. *Gateway to a Supernatural Life* is a guidebook to a deeper walk with the Holy Spirit, and it is as authentic as Jeff himself.

—*Stephen J. Avery*
Former running back, Pittsburgh Steelers
Avery Family Ministries, Pittsburgh, PA

Because Pastor Jeff Leake actually lives and breathes the book of Acts and is planting life-giving churches, the book you are holding in your hands is explosive. This isn't just a collection of eloquent and wise words, but a book that has the demonstrative and life-transforming power of the Jesus gospel on every page. This is more than just "desk" or "university" knowledge from a professor; it is well-tested and proven teaching from discipleship training and the frontier of evangelism. Read it, teach it, and see how the Holy Spirit will transform lives.

—*Johannes Amritzer*
Founder and President, Mission SOS International
Author, *How Jesus Healed the Sick: And How You Can Too!*

In this book, *Gateway to a Supernatural Life*, Jeff uses compelling biblical events and dramatic personal accounts to prove the power of the Holy Spirit can and still does make a difference in the lives of believers today. The Holy Spirit is God adding His super to our natural.

—*James Leake*
President, Acts 20:24 Ministries

Few issues are as important to Pentecostals as their personal experience in the life of the Spirit. There are also few issues that are as confusing to non-Pentecostals as this same experience. Jeff Leake approaches this subject in a thoughtful, biblical, and experiential way that I'm confident will remove much confusion and add much clarity to the importance of a dynamic Spirit-filled life for all believers. I would encourage individual and group study of this work, with the anticipation of a greater power for service for our Lord.

—*Stephen R. Tourville*
Superintendent, PennDel Network of the Assemblies of God
Coauthor, *Better Together: Harnessing the Power of Teamwork*

Pastor Jeff Leake writes a practical, eye-opening guide to accessing the supernatural power of the Holy Spirit. It's hard to imagine a more challenging and liberating exploration of this surprisingly unexplored area—the crucial role of the Holy Spirit in the lives of believers. *Gateway to a Supernatural Life* will bring you face-to-face with the limitless potential God has for you.

—*Brian Bolt*
Founder, CityReach Network
Lead Pastor, CityReach Church, Pittsburgh, PA
Author, *Reach: A Story of Multiplication in the City*

With the privilege of knowing Jeff personally, I have witnessed the power of miracles at work in his life's journey. *Gateway to a Supernatural Life* is a great bridge for conversation to discuss the supernatural reality of the life-changing experience of the baptism in the Holy Spirit. You will enjoy the story-strengthened, practical approach that gives anyone food for thought and opens the dialogue for interaction. As you read, enjoy your personal journey for the miracle God has in store for you.

—*Ron Heitman*
Lead Pastor, Evangel Church, Hanover Park, IL

I stand in awe of the simplicity, biblical integrity, and practicality of this book. Without a doubt, you are about to read one of the best books on the Holy Spirit; it is able to catapult any believer into a fruitful and adventurous Christian journey.

—*Fernando DeCarvalho*
Executive Director, SOS Adventure Office

I have been a pastor for over thirteen years and experienced the baptism in the Holy Spirit for the first time this past year at Jeff's church. As evidenced in this book, Jeff has a unique ability to make this beautiful and exciting Christian experience understandable and accessible to many Christians. I pray God will use this book to take everyday believers to new levels of worship, prayer, and service—to release a river of fervency from within every soul that encounters it.

—*Dr. Dan Muttart*
Pittsburgh, PA

Nothing will ignite your faith like the power of the Holy Spirit! And nothing will ignite your hunger like real-life stories. *Gateway to a Supernatural Life* will leave you longing and looking for your own "book of Acts" experience!

—*Ron Johnson*
Pastor, One Church, Orlando, FL

I grew up in churches that were alive with the tangible power of the Holy Spirit, and I'm eager to reproduce those experiences in our church today. I'm also eager to do it in a way that's sensitive to the seekers in our city who are exploring faith and giving church a shot. Jeff Leake has taught me how to introduce people to the transcendent presence of the Holy Spirit without being weird. This book is a gift for anyone who wants to experience the fullness of the Spirit in a culturally sensitive way.

—*Brad Leach*
Lead Pastor, CityLife Church, Philadelphia, PA

When I first heard that Jeff Leake was writing a book on the baptism in the Holy Spirit, I immediately said to myself, "Finally!" and for this simple reason: Jeff has an incredible gift to preach and teach on any given topic and make it easy to understand and apply. And since the book is about my favorite topic, I couldn't be happier! On every single page, Jeff makes you long for the power of the Holy Spirit over your life and for the ability to live a "book of Acts" lifestyle each day. Not only that, but he stirs up the faith in you that it is possible! I can't wait to see how many lives will be changed forever by reading *Gateway to a Supernatural Life*!

—*Samuel Strandberg*
Executive Director, Northeast Ministry School

In *Gateway to a Supernatural Life*, author Jeff Leake helps us take that beautiful, biblical, but often under-accessed gift of the baptism in the Holy Spirit off the shelf. In a clear, compelling way (and with life-in-the-real-world stories), Jeff removes the wrappings of confusion and controversy (and maybe even—dare I say it?—weirdness) to reveal the one thing our weak hearts have been longing for all along: Holy Spirit power to live the vivid Jesus-is-alive message in this broken world. Maybe the idea of Spirit baptism is brand-new to you. Or perhaps, like me, you need fresh eyes to see the vast potential for empowering transformation available to every believer through this gift from Jesus. Either way, *Gateway to a Supernatural Life* is for you.

—*Jodi Detrick*
Religion columnist for *The Seattle Times*
Author, *The Jesus-Hearted Woman*

I absolutely love this new book. Not only do I 100 percent believe in what Jeff is sharing, but I'm ecstatic that a contemporary leader and pastor has written a new book on the baptism in the Holy Spirit. The storytelling, theology, passion, quotes, and practical path Jeff lays out for anyone to receive the baptism in the Holy Spirit will make *Gateway to a Supernatural Life* an important book for many years to come. I plan on distributing it widely and promoting it enthusiastically because every Christian needs to read it.

—*Scott Hagan*
President, North Central University, Minneapolis, MN

Jeff Leake is an incredible communicator. He takes eternal truths and makes them accessible through practical insights and inspiring stories, always painting a clear path to personal transformation. But what really adds weight to what any author or communicator has to say is that person's testimony and spiritual fruit—and when you appraise Jeff's life, you see that he has fruit, and lots of it. I wholeheartedly recommend *Gateway to a Supernatural Life* because of the powerful truths clearly articulated that impart faith for Holy Spirit impact in your life and ministry. Get ready for God to add new chapters to your story as you experience His power for life.

—*Justin Maslanka*
Lead Pastor, CityReach Church, Cleveland, OH

GATEWAY TO A
SUPERNATURAL
LIFE

GATEWAY TO A
SUPERNATURAL
LIFE

THE INCREDIBLE POWER OF
HOLY SPIRIT BAPTISM

JEFF LEAKE

WHITAKER
HOUSE

GATEWAY TO A SUPERNATURAL LIFE:
The Incredible Power of Holy Spirit Baptism

Jeff Leake
allisonparkleadershipnetwork.com
jeffl@allisonparkchurch.com

ISBN: 978-1-64123-850-2
eBook ISBN: 978-1-64123-851-9
Printed in the United States of America
© 2017, 2022 by Jeff Leake

Whitaker House
1030 Hunt Valley Circle
New Kensington, PA 15068
www.whitakerhouse.com

LC record available at https://lccn.loc.gov/2022010494
LC ebook record available at https://lccn.loc.gov/2022010495

1 2 3 4 5 6 7 8 9 10 11   **W**   29 28 27 26 25 24 23 22

This book is dedicated to my parents, James and Rebecca Leake, who modeled for me so many things.

First of all, they allowed me to process all of my doubts and questions about the things of God without ever being threatened. They patiently answered me and let me struggle with my doubts and hesitations about how the Holy Spirit works.

Second, they demonstrated for me a humble heart of love and service for people.

Third, they live a life marked by the power of God. I grew up hearing stories of God's healing power at work in people's lives as a specific result of my father's prayers.

Finally, my parents demonstrated to me faithfulness to each other for over fifty years, and to the local church they pastored for forty years.

I will be forever thankful for your role in my life.

CONTENTS

FOREWORD

I remember reading a book by Dr. Francis Schaeffer when I was a young man, and he asked this question: "If the Holy Spirit was taken from you tomorrow morning, what difference would it make in your life?" He then went on to recount all the ways he was helped by the Holy Spirit on a daily basis. He finished by saying, "I believe I would physically die if the Holy Spirit were to be taken out of my life tomorrow." When I was a young man, that statement rattled me! I suppose it took added years and an added lifelong desperation for the Holy Spirit to empower me in order for me to come to the same conclusion. In time I came to agree with Dr. Schaeffer, and I attribute it all to the experience of being baptized in the Holy Spirit. My reliance on the Holy Spirit didn't stop there with a single act, but His power continued to flourish in and through me.

As I read through my friend Jeff Leake's book, my heart was warmed. Not only in a very practical way, but in a deeply spiritual way, Pastor Leake answers the most-asked questions concerning the baptism in the Holy Spirit.

Remember that all of the writers of the New Testament were baptized in the Holy Spirit and spoke in tongues. There were not the arguments against speaking in other tongues then as there are today.

Pastor Leake also tackles the most difficult questions on the baptism in the Holy Spirit with love and humility, which leaves the reader with well-thought-out answers. His experiences and stories are fascinating, and you'll note that his wife is very much a part of this husband/wife commitment to the ministry of the Holy Spirit in their lives and in the life of the church they pastor.

If you have not experienced the baptism of the Holy Spirit, you will understand how He is the SUPER that turns our natural into the SUPERNATURAL by the time you have finished reading! Perhaps the baptism in the Holy Spirit is what you have been missing. I believe that after reading *Gateway to a Supernatural Life*, you will seek for the baptism in the Holy Spirit. Remember, this baptism is offered as a gift from our Lord and Savior. If you've already been baptized in the Holy Spirit, you will desire to move into a deeper walk of supernatural power. With all of my heart I implore you to KEEP READING!

—*Dr. Rich Wilkerson*
Pastor, Trinity Church Miami, FL

INTRODUCTION

When I sat down to write about this topic, I was amazed by just how little has been written over the years about the baptism in the Holy Spirit—especially since entire denominations and church movements have been shaped by this experience. Yet few writers have attempted to explain the practical value and biblical reasoning behind this important moment in a believer's spiritual journey.

People may avoid this topic for several reasons. First of all, *it's controversial*. There are so many strong feelings about when the baptism in the Holy Spirit occurs, how it happens, and what evidence demonstrates that it has happened in a believer's life. For some it has become a dividing line, of sorts, for defining fellowship. Many believers take the stance that if another person doesn't agree with their position on the matter, they don't want to have anything to do with him or her.

In my opinion, that kind of attitude is not only unbiblical, it's downright silly.

We need to leave room for others to disagree with us. Our choice of who we love, do life with, and minister beside should never be defined or limited by variances of opinion on matters like this. We have to be bigger and better than that. While it can be pleasant to be surrounded with likeminded believers, we don't enrich true fellowship when we avoid a controversial subject. I always learn from those with whom I disagree. My hope is that this book will be a source of good discussion and interaction, regardless of whether you agree with everything written here.

The second reason people avoid this topic has to do with both *awkwardness* and *confusion*. Maybe for you, the last few paragraphs meant absolutely nothing. Not only are you unaware of any controversy, but you are also not at all familiar with the experience. The biggest reaction from those who are new to the concept of the baptism in the Holy Spirit happens when they hear the phrase "speaking in tongues." The blank looks on their faces say it all: "What are you even talking about?"

Those who do know the meaning of the term *tongues* often aren't sure how to explain it to someone who has questions. What they have experienced personally might even confuse their thinking compared to what they themselves were taught. For all these reasons, there's an inevitable sense of awkwardness whenever the topic comes up.

A few months ago, I was standing in line at a coffee shop that I frequent. The baristas there know that I'm a pastor. When I come into the store, they greet me by saying, "Hey, Pastor Jeff,'" which is always funny because the entire room turns to see the "holy man" who just entered the coffee shop. Well, on this particular morning, one of the girls added something to the greeting: "Hey, Pastor Jeff, we were waiting for you because we have a question. What is this deal about 'speaking in tongues'?"

Talk about being put on the spot!

As far as I know, none of these employees are believers. This particular barista asked this question, loudly, in front of a full store. (It was around quarter to seven in the morning, and the line to get coffee was long.) I had thirty seconds to answer while they filled my order for a grande dark roast. What in the world could I even say in such a short time and in such a public forum?

Here's what I said: "We believe God does miracles, which are events that can't be explained as natural phenomena. Do you believe that?"

"Yes, I believe God can do miracles," each replied.

I looked around to see everyone around me in line leaning in and nodding their heads. Then I added, "Speaking in tongues is just a miracle of language. God prompts a person to speak a language they have never learned as a sign that He is at work in a situation. I know that sounds kind of out there, but you can imagine if someone spoke to you in English and they had never studied it, that would be a pretty convincing sign that God was talking to you."

They all laughed, nodded their heads at my explanation, and seemed satisfied. I could tell that what I had said was all they were ready to hear at the moment. So I picked up my coffee, sat down in my normal seat, and sipped my drink.

I have found that many people are curious and yet confused about this subject of "speaking in tongues." The baptism in the Holy Spirit involves a discussion about speaking in tongues, but it involves so much more than that. In fact, the baptism in the Holy Spirit is truly the gateway to living a supernatural life. God is a God of miracles. He wants to do miracles in and through each of us.

That's why this topic is so important. But the controversy and the sense of awkward confusion surrounding it seem to prevent us from having an open and intentional discussion about how to be true to ourselves while living a supernatural life. I have had many conversations with young church leaders who have serious questions not only about the biblical nature of this experience, but also about the practical value of it. The questions they have are as follows: "What does it do? Why is it necessary? And why can't we have a serious dialogue about this and about how it fits into our lives and ministries?"

I want to get the dialogue started. I also want to teach the value of this experience for every believer. My passion is to see every person who believes in Jesus come to an understanding of how God can use them to experience miracles. I want every believer to understand who they are in Christ and who the Holy Spirit is within their lives. Too many believers are living out of their own strength and wisdom. They don't understand who lives within them and what He is capable of doing for and through them.

As you read this book, don't read it to resolve a controversy or solve some sense of awkward confusion. Read this book to come to grips with the supernatural potential within your life. Read it with a hunger to see God do all He is able to do through your life. Read it with an open mind to discover things about your mission as a person that you may never have known before. As you read this book, hopefully you will pick up on three things regarding my writing/teaching style:

It's Scripture-based: My goal is to base every principle in every chapter on something the Bible teaches. We can discover so much about the baptism in the Holy Spirit from what was written in the New Testament. My desire is to write accurately and practically about what the Bible clearly declares we can expect and believe.

It's story-oriented: I learn best through the lives of others. So when I consider a biblical concept, I want to see how that concept expresses itself in the real world and in the lives of everyday people. In each chapter I tell at least one story about how the baptism in the Holy Spirit has made an impact on someone's life in a powerful way.

It's simple: I can hold a discussion about deep theological truths with those who want to dive into the more profound and precise aspects of theological interpretation, but my gift is to take what is complicated and explain it in the simplest of terms so that everyone can understand and apply what is written.

If you're looking for an overtly theological treatment of the subject, this isn't the book that will accomplish that goal. It's designed to be practical and motivational. This book is for people who know little or nothing about the baptism in the Holy Spirit; it's also for those who want to look at the subject in a fresh way.

I hope that once you have read this book, you will have had a personal experience with God. You'll have a greater understanding of your Best Friend, the Holy Spirit; you'll see the potential for God to work through your life to release supernatural things into your world; and you'll be able to explain what you have experienced based on Bible passages that address this work of God.

May you be blessed as you begin this journey.

ONE
IT'S MORE THAN ENOUGH

*Take the Holy Spirit out of the equation of my life, and it
would spell b-o-r-i-n-g. Add Him to the equation of your life,
and anything can happen.*
—Mark Batterson[1]

Without the baptism in the Holy Spirit, what we have is simply not enough!

This is the conclusion Jesus's disciples would have reached when they heard Him make this statement: *"Do not leave Jerusalem, but wait for the gift my Father promised, which you have heard me speak about. For John baptized with water, but in a few days you will be baptized with the Holy Spirit"* (Acts 1:4–5). Consider the whirlwind of change that Peter, James, John, and the others had just been through.

Only weeks earlier, they had watched their leader as He was nailed to a cross. For three years, they had followed this revolutionary leader, Jesus of Nazareth. While Jesus had predicted the moment of His death, biblical history reveals that the disciples were personally and emotionally unprepared to face it. Their

Messiah was crucified. He died. Friends took His body down from the cross and buried Him in a tomb.

All seemed hopeless. Nothing made sense. The disciples hid away, afraid that their own lives were in danger.

Then came Sunday!

Jesus rose. The stone was rolled away. The dead body of their Master came back to life, and they saw Him in His resurrected form. Talk about a game changer! If this was possible, then anything was possible! People don't just come back from the dead. But Jesus did! He conquered death. He overcame the grave, and in so doing, He proved that He was who He said He was.

Acts 1:3 tells us, *"After his suffering, he presented himself to them* [the disciples] *and gave many convincing proofs that he was alive. He appeared to them over a period of forty days and spoke about the kingdom of God."*

During this forty-day period of time, Jesus began to unfold to His disciples what He wanted them to do next. His mission for them, should they accept it, was to take the message of His resurrection to the entire planet. Every person, every race, every nation was not only to hear about what had happened but was also to be invited into a personal relationship with God through Jesus Christ: *"Go and make disciples of all nations, baptizing them in the name of the Father and of the Son and of the Holy Spirit, and teaching them to obey everything I have commanded you"* (Matthew 28:19–20).

Can you imagine? If you have listened to teachings from the Bible, you have probably heard these famous verses. The challenge Jesus gave to His disciples is often referred to as the Great Commission. But when you think of the implications of this commission, it seems to be more like a *huge impossibility.*

+ Most of these disciples weren't formally educated.

+ Many of them were in their early twenties—some in their late teens.

+ All of them lived in a very poor region under the domination of Roman rule.

+ For most of the three years they had walked with Jesus, the twelve disciples hadn't gotten along very well.

+ Several of them were rivals and were battling for top position in this discipleship group.

+ None of them had traveled more than a few hundred miles from home.

+ All this took place in an era of limited technology. Travel was by horse or on foot. There were no phones, tweets, emails, or even an established Pony Express.

Now Jesus expected them to take over the world!

By the way, we should mention that He wanted them to do all of this *without Him.* Just after He gave this commission, He disappeared. *"After he said this, he was taken up before their very eyes, and a cloud hid him from their sight"* (Acts 1:9).

What we have in our lives without the power of the Holy Spirit is simply *not enough!*

Can you identify with that reality? Every one of us faces things in our lives that cause us to admit, "What I have right now is simply not enough!"

+ Addictions we have tried and failed to overcome

+ Depressing circumstances that constantly drag us down

+ Complications with our family relationships that leave us frustrated and confused

+ Habits we just can't seem to break

+ Needs we just can't meet

- ✦ Visions and dreams we want to pursue but can't see how they'll become a reality

- ✦ Even our attempts to follow Christ faithfully often feel hollow and lacking; we feel like we don't measure up. We slot the life we want to live into the "huge impossibility" category and feel powerless and inadequate to do anything about it.

If you have felt that way, I have some really good news for you: God knows you aren't adequate for the task *in your own strength*. Your inadequacy doesn't surprise Him. It doesn't shake His confidence in you or in His plans for your life. It doesn't limit what He can do in and through you.

In fact, becoming aware of our own personal inadequacy *must* happen before God can do powerful things in our lives. Jesus taught this principle in His famous Sermon on the Mount: *"Blessed are the poor in spirit, for theirs is the kingdom of heaven"* (Matthew 5:3). We could paraphrase that statement like this: *Nothing will change in my life until I'm willing to admit that I need help.*

Before we go on in this chapter, why don't you stop and read that last sentence out loud to yourself. How did you feel? Do you agree with what you said? Did you resist this thought? It's critically important that we accept this truth before we can move forward to make changes in our lives.

You must recognize your need for something more before God can release something amazing in and through your life. Self-dependency is the enemy of a supernatural life, the life God has in mind for you. Think about that word *supernatural*. I define it as "above and beyond what is naturally possible." It involves accessing a power that is not within our natural selves. It describes what happens when God gets involved with people who are willing to trust Him.

THE POWER OF THE HOLY SPIRIT CHANGED PETER'S LIFE

Consider Simon Peter, one of the disciples. He was part of the inner circle of Jesus's discipleship group. There were twelve disciples, and Jesus spent the most time with three of them: Peter, James, and John. Peter's life serves as a picture of what God wants to do in our lives. Consider the following points.

PETER TRIED TO SERVE GOD IN HIS OWN STRENGTH.

There's probably no better moment that defines Simon Peter than the moment he promised Jesus undying loyalty. It was just after the Last Supper. Jesus had predicted that He would be betrayed and that everyone in the room would forsake Him at His moment of greatest need. Simon Peter spoke up with all the self-confidence he could muster: *"Even if all fall away on account of you, I never will"* (Matthew 26:33). And again he pledged, *"Even if I have to die with you, I will never disown you"* (verse 35).

When Simon Peter made these promises to Jesus, I believe he was being serious. He truly meant to follow through, but he had no idea how weak he actually was and how strong his desire for self-preservation would be. When the moment of truth came, Peter denied even knowing Jesus, not once but three times. (See John 18:15–18, 25–27.)

PETER WAS INCONSISTENT IN HIS EFFORTS, AT BEST.

This wasn't the first time Simon Peter had demonstrated his good intentions and inconsistent results.

- One minute he was walking on the water with Jesus; the next moment he was sinking in the waves, overwhelmed by fear. (See Matthew 14:22–34.)
- One minute he was making the greatest confession ever (that Jesus is the Son of God); the next minute he was rebuking

Jesus to His face for even considering the mission of dying on the cross. (See Matthew 16:13–28.)

+ One minute he was standing boldly in the garden of Gethsemane, sword in hand, attacking the men trying to arrest Jesus. The next minute, he was calling curses down on himself while he denied ever knowing Jesus. (See Matthew 26:50–56, 69–75.)

Don't you just love this guy! I appreciate Simon Peter because I see so much of myself in him. He meant well. He even did well from time to time. But then his own sinful, selfish nature took over, and he couldn't sustain the forward momentum in his life.

EVENTUALLY, PETER FAILED MISERABLY AND DESPAIRED OF LIFE.

The Bible tells us that when Simon Peter uttered his third denial, a rooster crowed. It was just as Jesus had predicted. *"This very night, before the rooster crows, you will disown me three times"* (Matthew 26:34).

What a terrible moment! Can you see it? Peter insisted to the servant girl who inquired of his connection to Christ, "I swear to you, I don't know the man!" Right at that moment, as the dawn was ready to break, the rooster cried out. Peter looked up, remembering what Jesus had predicted. He glanced over to where Jesus was on trial for His life. There, Peter's eyes met the eyes of his friend and master. What deep sadness he must have seen in Jesus's eyes. Luke 22:62 tells us that Simon Peter *"went outside and wept bitterly."*

Have you been there? Face-to-face with your own failure? Overcome by the sorrow of your own selfish behavior? Despairing of life because you see the despicable nature of your own heart?

Simon Peter sobbed. You know the kind of emotional response where the tears flow from deep inside your being. Tears spilled from his eyes, ran down his face, and dripped off his nose. Deep sobs. Gut-wrenching groans. Uncontrollable tears. Everything seemed over. Nothing had meaning. He never, ever imagined that he would fail in this way. Not only had he failed his friend at this time of greatest need, but he had failed in front of the entire world. What humiliation...embarrassment...shame...and despair!

Unlike Judas, another disciple who had failed, Simon Peter decided to move on from this moment. Judas felt there was no hope for his life after he betrayed Jesus for thirty pieces of silver. Judas believed he could never be forgiven, that he was beyond redemption; so he took his own life. Somehow, Peter pushed beyond his despair and kept moving forward.

Coming face-to-face with our own selfishness and sinfulness is life-altering, but it's a necessary step for someone who is going to be used by God.

FEAR AND DISILLUSIONMENT STOLE PETER'S CONFIDENCE AND REDUCED HIS VISION FOR THE FUTURE.

Simon Peter didn't take his own life like Judas did. But the gospel of John records Peter's struggle with shame and despair:

- ✦ He hid in fear—afraid that the Jewish religious leaders would kill him too. (See John 20:19.)

- ✦ He decided to leave "ministry" and return to his known trade of fishing. (See John 21:3.)

- ✦ His confidence was shaken. When the resurrected Jesus asked him, "Simon, do you love Me?" Peter could hardly muster an answer, "*Yes, Lord, you know that I love you*" (John 21:16).

Can you imagine the great loss to the church if Simon Peter had remained lost in despair? Thankfully, he moved on, and Jesus forgave him. If you read John 21, you will find amazing grace and acceptance as Christ gave Peter a second chance. Jesus assured the disciple that his life still counted; that there was a purpose for his life and God still wanted to use him. However, it wasn't until the day of Pentecost that Simon Peter truly stepped into new power and vision for his life.

NOT ONLY WAS PETER RESTORED FROM HIS PAST—HE WAS FILLED WITH GOD'S OVERCOMING POWER.

The moment we read about in Luke 22:62 could have been the end for Simon Peter. The account of how he wept bitterly after his three denial of Jesus could have been the final word regarding his life. If he had remained overwhelmed by his shame, we would not have one more word to read about his life. He wouldn't have been one of the pillars of the early church. He would have stayed stuck in the shame of his past.

But Simon Peter didn't allow his failure to become final!

When Jesus rose, He made it His mission to forgive Simon Peter. Jesus pursued Peter and made sure the disciple knew that the past was in the past, and that the past didn't limit the potential or purpose of his future. Peter was forgiven. Peter was restored. He didn't have to live in shame. He had a future; he had hope.

But even that wasn't enough!

God couldn't have used Simon Peter like He did in Jerusalem (see Acts 2) if Peter hadn't been baptized in the Holy Spirit. Forgiveness was critical to Peter, but it wasn't enough. He needed restoration, but that wasn't enough. Simon Peter needed more. He needed to be infused with and empowered by the Holy Spirit.

WHEN PETER WAS BAPTIZED IN THE HOLY SPIRIT, HIS LIFE RADICALLY CHANGED.

Acts 2 provides the record of Simon Peter's transformation. He was in the upper room praying with the 120 when God poured out the Holy Spirit upon them all. Along with the others in the room, Peter heard the sound of a rushing wind and saw the huge flames of fire that came into the room and broke into 120 smaller flames that came to rest above the head of each person.

God's Spirit so impacted these people that they all began to speak out loud in prayer. Peter was right there in the middle of it all as the Holy Spirit filled them to overflowing. The noise was so loud and the commotion so great that the people gathered in the streets outside the house were bewildered by what was going on.

About that time, *"Peter stood up...and addressed the crowd"* (Acts 2:14). Simon Peter, the disciple who had denied Jesus just a few weeks before, took the lead! This was the same guy who could hardly speak when Jesus asked, "Do you love Me?"—the same guy who had been hiding in a room, terrified that the religious leaders would arrest him.

There he was, standing boldly in front of several thousand people, declaring to them that Jesus was alive. Remember, this was the same city where Jesus had been crucified. Peter was speaking just a mile or two from the place where the crucifixion had occurred. He was preaching to some of the same people who had yelled, "Crucify Him!" when Jesus was on trial before Pilate. Simon Peter was risking his life by taking a stand at that moment.

But because he had been baptized in the Holy Spirit, he had the strength and courage to do what had not been possible for him to do before.

GOD RELEASED SUPERNATURAL POWER THROUGH PETER'S LIFE.

Supernatural things started to happen for Peter and through Peter.

The book of Acts records how the Holy Spirit impacts the life of someone like Simon Peter. In fact, the official title of the book is The Acts of the Apostles, which we might rephrase as The Acts of the Holy Spirit—*Through* the Lives of the Apostles. Peter was baptized in the Holy Spirit, and this marked the beginning of the supernatural in his ministry.

+ He preached with great power, and 3,000 people were saved in one day. (See Acts 2:14-41.)

+ He prayed for a crippled man who was healed. (See Acts 3:1–10.)

+ He spoke boldly while on trial in front of the Sanhedrin, the same court that had so terrified him before. (See Acts 4:1–22.)

+ Mighty miracles happened as crowds brought their sick to him for prayer. (See Acts 5:12–16.)

+ He prayed for a crippled man who began to walk. (See Acts 9:32–35.)

+ He prayed for a dead woman, and she came back to life. (See Acts 9:36–42.)

+ He received a vision during prayer that changed the way the church leaders thought about the Gentiles who needed the gospel. (See Acts 10:9–48.)

+ God sent an angel to break him out of prison, where he was being held for preaching about the resurrected Jesus. (See Acts 12:1–19.)

Remember, this was the same guy who had denied Jesus and cowered in fear. On his own, he was inconsistent and ineffective. He was self-consumed and full of pride, but Jesus changed all that. Jesus forgave him and restored him. And when the Holy Spirit came upon Peter, he was transformed into a man who was bold, powerful, consistent, and filled with joy.

We simply can't overestimate the value of Simon Peter's experience with the Holy Spirit. He was never the same after he was baptized in the Holy Spirit. What he had before Acts 2 wasn't enough! He needed more. He needed to be empowered by the

Holy Spirit. God took him from ordinary and inconsistent, and transformed him into someone who stepped into supernatural miracles that affected the entire world.

This is the will of God for your life!

What you have today is not enough, but the power of the Holy Spirit is enough! God has called you to so much more. His plan for you is to do so much more than just survive another week. He wants to use you to do the supernatural. Yes, you! He wants the Holy Spirit to be manifested in and released through your life. What you have been doesn't have to determine what you will be. Your past doesn't define your potential.

But what you are in yourself just isn't enough. You need more. You need to be baptized in the Holy Spirit. He provides the power you need for your life, and that power is more than enough!

CHAPTER ONE DISCUSSION QUESTIONS

1. Describe a time in your life when you knew that what you had just wasn't enough.

2. Can you imagine what the disciples felt when Jesus unexpectedly ascended into heaven and left them here on earth without Him? What words would you use to describe the emotions they likely felt?

3. When you see someone who turns their life around, how does that motivate to you? In what ways does that give you hope?

4. When you consider the life of Simon Peter, what role did the Holy Spirit play in the radical transformation of his life?

5. In what area of your life do you most need the help of the Holy Spirit?

TWO
IT'S VISIBLE

*I want to live so that I am truly submitted to the Spirit's
leading on a daily basis. Christ said it is better for us that the
Spirit came, and I want to live like I know that is true.
I don't want to keep crawling when I have the ability to fly.*
—Francis Chan[2]

Some things only change under the influence of the Holy Spirit.

For Brian Bolt, his first defining moment happened in the back of an ambulance. The year was 2002, Brian was twenty-three years old, and his life had been in a self-destructive free fall. Arrested for drug use at the age of sixteen, Brian was given the opportunity to serve out his sentence by enlisting in the Navy rather than spending his days in the prison system.

The Navy was good for Brian. He got his GED, received training in his area of gifting, and obtained the discipline and structure necessary for a life free from drug use. However, the inner drive to use and abuse drugs never went away, and before long Brian was back at it again while in port in San Diego, California. Friends invited Brian to cross the border into Mexico, where he found the opportunity to dive headlong into not only drug use but an entire drug industry.

Brian went AWOL, and he even used his Navy ID to help him carry drugs across the border as a drug mule. He was compensated in both money and all the drugs he could ever hope to consume. For several years Brian was in and out of the brig, and in and out of serious trouble in many ways. His life was spiraling out of control, and he was taking increasingly dangerous risks.

One day, back in his hometown of Cumberland, Maryland, Brian ended up in a bad situation.

"I got caught trying to rob a guy," he reports, "and when the guy found out, he took a swing at me. I swung back, and knocked him to the ground. The second guy came at me, and as I was in the process of fighting him off, the first man got up off of the floor and pulled a gun. He pointed it at my head, and fired."

Blood filled the barroom floor. The bullet pinballed inside of Brian's skull and landed in his carotid artery, which slowed the bleeding enough for him to survive.

Brian recounts that moment: "As I lay there on the floor realizing what had happened to me, I remember feeling relieved. There was nothing in life worth living for. I was so empty. I think I wanted to die."

Paramedics came and wheeled him into an ambulance.

As the vehicle rushed toward the hospital, the EMT turned to Brian and said, "Son, you're probably going to die. Do you know Jesus as your Savior?"

"No," Brian replied.

The paramedic asked softly, "Would you like to pray with me right now to give your life to Christ?"

Brian says, "At that moment, something tugged at my heart and I knew that was what I needed in my life." So there, in the back of that ambulance, Brian prayed and invited Jesus to take over his life.

For seventy-five days, Brian was in and out of a medically induced coma. Doctors performed multiple surgeries not only to save his life but also to re-create the entire left side of his face. Only the grace of God and the skillful hands of the surgeons saved Brian's life. When he was released from the hospital, he knew something had happened to him when he prayed to receive Christ, but he had no idea what to do with his newfound faith. He went back to the streets and started hanging out with the same old group.

But God had a plan for Brian Bolt. One day while Brian was hanging out on the streets of San Diego, a group of guys from a Victory Outreach Men's Home approached him.

"God has a plan for your life," they told Brian. "We have a place for you. If you come with us, we will help you learn what it is to live for God and to live for His purpose." Brian agreed to go with them. He entered the Men's Home, a free recovery home provided by Victory Outreach Church with the goal of helping men and women get free from drugs and discipling them as followers of Christ.

One of the conditions of living in the Home was participation in Bible studies and prayer meetings several times a day. Participants learned the basics of following Christ. Brian started reading the Bible. He learned about prayer. And one day, during a prayer session, some of the guys laid their hands on Brian, and he was baptized in the Holy Spirit.

Just like the Bible describes this experience in Acts 2:1–4, Brian was filled with the Holy Spirit and began to pray in a spiritual language. (We'll talk about this in a later chapter.)

"When they prayed for me, I felt a surge of peace and power rush through my entire being," Brian says. "The emotional intensity of this moment was greater than any high I had ever experienced on drugs. Whatever this was, I wanted as much of it as I possibly could get!"

IT'S A CONTAGIOUS FREEDOM

Now let me tell you the rest of Brian's story. Shortly after being baptized in the Holy Spirit, he felt called to be a pastor. So he enrolled in the training he needed to reach his goal. In 2005, he joined the staff at Allison Park Church with the express intent of planting a church in the city of Pittsburgh that would be targeted to reach drug addicts, the broken, the formerly incarcerated, and those in need of hope.

Not only did Brian effectively plant CityReach Church Pittsburgh, but he has also led the way in helping to establish CityReach churches all over the United States. Many of these churches began with the establishment of a Hope Home, a free recovery home for people who have tried everything and have nowhere else to go. These homes have given hundreds of addicts a chance for a new life and a fresh start.

So what role does the baptism in the Holy Spirit play in helping people break free of addiction? What role did it play in Brian Bolt's life? What role does it play in the function of the Hope Homes, where so many are being set free?

When you are filled with the Holy Spirit, His mighty power influences your thoughts, actions, and feelings.

"The baptism in the Holy Spirit is the key experience for an addict," Brian says. "Prior to that, you are fighting those old cravings out of your own effort and determination. But when the Holy Spirit fills you, you have a source of peace that overpowers everything else. Once I was baptized in the Holy Spirit, I felt a level of satisfaction in my soul that almost totally eliminated the magnetism of the old addictive cravings."

When describing the strategy of CityReach, Brian explains, "Not only do we want to bring people to a saving understanding of Jesus in their lives, but we also want to get them baptized in the Holy Spirit as soon as possible. As soon as a Hope Home resident is baptized in the Holy Spirit, everything about managing and leading them becomes so much easier. They have Someone inside of them giving them the power to overcome."

This powerful approach to freedom is described in the Bible. Look at what the apostle Paul wrote in his letter to the Ephesians:

> Be very careful, then, how you live—not as unwise but as wise, making the most of every opportunity, because the days are evil. Therefore do not be foolish, but understand what the Lord's will is. Do not get drunk on wine, which leads to debauchery. Instead, be filled with the Spirit, speaking to one another with psalms, hymns, and songs from the Spirit. Sing and make music from your heart to the Lord, always giving thanks to God the Father for everything, in the name of our Lord Jesus Christ. (Ephesians 5:15–20)

Notice how these verses relate to our lives today:

+ We live in evil days with temptations and trouble lurking all around us—circumstances that call for us to live carefully and with great wisdom.

+ It's foolish to allow ourselves to come under the influence of alcohol (or other substances) to the point of drunkenness because it leads us toward debauchery, which means the kind of self-destructive behavior that results from life being out of control—a life that makes us feel debased, ashamed, filled with regret.

+ It isn't God's will that we experience that kind of pain. He has a better plan for us than a life filled with regret.

♦ It is God's will that we *be filled with the Spirit*, which leads to a life filled with peace and joy, and a life free of regret.

Compare the effects of drugs and alcohol and the impact of the Holy Spirit: both have an influential effect on us. When you drink or use drugs, that substance affects your thoughts, your feelings, and your actions. When you are filled with the Holy Spirit, His mighty power influences your thoughts, actions, and feelings. For example, drinking alcohol to excess or using mind-altering substances impairs judgment and causes behavior that is potentially destructive. Being filled with the Holy Spirit improves judgment and inspires life-giving behavior.

We need to be filled with the Holy Spirit! This experience is something more than what happens to us when we accept Jesus as our Savior. At that moment, we receive the Holy Spirit within our lives. In fact, we can't be saved apart from the regenerating work of the Holy Spirit. *"But because of his great love for us, God, who is rich in mercy, made us alive with Christ even when we were dead in transgressions—it is by grace you have been saved"* (Ephesians 2:4–5).

For those who believe in Jesus, that initial moment of Holy Spirit infusion is not the end of His work in our lives; it's just the beginning. The phrase in Ephesians 5:18, *"be filled with the Spirit,"* actually reads like this in the original Greek: "Be being [constantly and continually] filled with the Holy Spirit." If we pursue the will of God, we will seek to bring our lives under the constant and continuous infilling of the Holy Spirit. This implies that we must cultivate a relationship with the Holy Spirit.

When we are baptized in the Holy Spirit, His infilling is an overpowering influence that improves our judgment and gives overflowing life to our souls. You see, some changes can only happen under the ongoing influence of the Holy Spirit. Some habits are just too hard to break in our own strength. Some tendencies are just too powerful to overcome. Some hurts are just too deep to process. Some pain is just too intense to move beyond.

But when the Holy Spirit fills our lives, habits break. Temptations are overcome. Hurts are healed. Pain no longer dominates. The filling of the Holy Spirit is like a jet engine that propels an airplane to break the pull of gravity, lifting the heavy weight of that plane into the sky, thousands of feet into the air. It would be impossible for that airplane to break free of gravity without the engine. In a similar way, we need the power of the Holy Spirit to help us break free of the "gravity" of sin and despair and destructive habits.

IT'S A VISIBLE CHANGE

Let me tell you how the Holy Spirit totally changed my grandfather's life. Thomas Leake worked in the coal mines as a boy because his father was an alcoholic and couldn't support his family. Thomas brought his paycheck home every week and handed it over to his mother so the family would have money for food. Because he was working, he had to quit school at an early age, which created a deep-seated anger and frustration that he had hit a dead end so early in life.

After he married my grandmother, they moved onto a piece of land, started a farm on the side, and began to raise a family.

My dad (his son) recalls, "He was a hard man: angry all the time, always in a fight, a chain-smoker, depressed. He never went to church and had little use for the things of God."

Each day he went off to work. While eating his lunch in the cafeteria, he would drink coffee from a company mug. When he finished the coffee, he slipped the mug into his lunch bucket. He did this daily, stealing mugs until the family had a large collection at home. The family never knew the mugs were stolen.

One day, someone invited him to a revival meeting. When the speaker gave the altar call, my grandfather shocked everyone who knew him when he walked to the front to surrender his life to Christ.

Shortly after his conversion, Thomas Leake was baptized in the Holy Spirit. This baptism had several effects on my grandfather's life. First of all, it gave him the power to quit smoking. Shortly after experiencing the outpouring of the Holy Spirit in his life, he felt prompted to throw every cigarette he owned and his tobacco and pipe into the coal-burning stove. He never touched tobacco again.

Second, he felt convicted about his petty thefts. One night, shortly after his Holy Spirit baptism, my grandmother looked in the cupboard and couldn't find a single mug. When she asked my grandfather about this, he confessed what he had done and told her he had taken everything he had ever stolen back to the company, confessed to his foreman, and made things right before God.

Third, the anger in his life disappeared. The frustration was gone. He stopped fighting. He even became a bit tender and was often touched to the point of tears when hearing a story about the grace of God in someone's life. He not only raised his family to love God, but he served as a lay preacher at several outreaches around the town. God took a man who was filled with anger and transformed him into a man who was filled with peace and under the influence of the Holy Spirit.

This transformation had a powerful impact on my dad. In fact, it was a significant factor in his deciding to go into the ministry. He saw a miraculous change happen in his own family, and he wanted God to use him to help others experience that same kind of change. This is the result of being filled with the Holy Spirit.

IT ALL BEGINS WITH WORSHIP

The challenge of Ephesians 5:18 is to be continually and constantly filled with the Holy Spirit. That sounds great! We want

God's will to be fulfilled in our lives. We don't want a life filled with debauchery and regret. We want a life that is filled with power and peace and life. How does that happen? Paul provides some advice that is by now familiar:

> *Be filled with the Spirit, speaking to one another with psalms, hymns, and songs from the Spirit. Sing and make music from your heart to the Lord, always giving thanks to God the Father for everything, in the name of our Lord Jesus Christ.*
> (Ephesians 5:18–20)

"Be filled with the Spirit" is the command. The process recommended for this then immediately follows: *"speaking to one another with psalms, hymns, and songs from the Spirit"* (spontaneous singing from the heart). Then Paul adds, *"Sing and make music from your heart to the Lord, always giving thanks to God the Father for everything."*

Paul's words are filled with wisdom. First, the Holy Spirit is attracted to our choice to worship. When we declare the value and worth of God and we recognize the person and power of Jesus, we join forces with the Holy Spirit. You see, the Holy Spirit's primary work in the world is to bring glory and honor to Jesus. So anytime we choose to honor Jesus, we magnetize our hearts to attract the presence of the Holy Spirit.

Second, the Holy Spirit draws close to us as we choose to worship. Remember that the Holy Spirit is the third person of the Trinity. He is every bit as much God as the Father and Jesus are. When we worship, He draws near to us in a real and tangible way. *"You are holy, enthroned in the praises of* [Your people]*"* (Psalm 22:3 NKJV). As we worship, it's as though He steps into the room and rests upon our hearts as His throne.

Third, the Holy Spirit is released within and around us as we worship. The verses in Ephesians tell us that we are to sing songs out of our spirit and to make music in our hearts. Notice that the emphasis is on our hearts. We are spiritual beings. The center of our body is the place where our spirit resides. So, we sing or praise out of the depths of our being.

Jesus promised this in John 7:37–39, "'*Let anyone who is thirsty come to me and drink. Whoever believes in me, as Scripture has said, rivers of living water will flow from within them.' By this he meant the Spirit, whom those who believed in him were later to receive.*"

"*Rivers of living water will flow **from within** them.*" As we worship, we release the river of living water that resides within us. As we vocalize our praise, an explosion of life is released from the center of our person. We feel the rush of God's presence being released out of our hearts, through our lips, and overflowing into our lives. It's powerful.

Notice that the recommended actions of Ephesians 5:18–20 are vocal: sing, make music, speak to one another, give thanks. The process of being filled with the Spirit requires that we speak, sing, and declare things out loud from our lips. When we vocalize our praise, we release something out of our spirits. The Holy Spirit is released out of our inner being, like a flood or a raging river, as we speak forth our praise to God.

Why don't we start there right now? Before we go any further with this discussion about the baptism in the Holy Spirit, let's begin by vocalizing our worship. Find a quiet place where you feel comfortable praying out loud and confess this prayer to God:

God, I thank You for who You are in my life. You are the Creator of the universe. You are the Sustainer of my life. In You, I find everything that I need.

Jesus, I thank You for dying on the cross for me. Thank You for shedding Your blood to pay for my sin. Thank You for Your resurrection. I declare that You are alive and that You are doing an amazing work in the world and in my life.

Holy Spirit, I invite You to take over my life. Thank You for helping me worship. I open my heart to You. Have Your way in my life. Fill me. Overflow me. Release the raging river of life within my soul. In Jesus's name, amen.

CHAPTER TWO DISCUSSION QUESTIONS

1. When you look back on your life, who has had the greatest positive influence on you? What made that person so influential?

2. Read Ephesians 5:15–20. There are times when drugs, alcohol, and even certain relationships can have an unhealthy influence on us. What are some negative effects of unhealthy influences?

3. How is the Holy Spirit the best influence you could ever experience?

4. Read John 7:37–39. What do you picture when you hear Jesus's description?

5. The chapter in Ephesians 5 teach us that the Holy Spirit is activated when we start to worship. If you are going through a challenging time in your life, one choice is to worship. If you don't worship, what other choices could you make?

6. What one thing will you do after this to activate the Holy Spirit in your life?

THREE

IT'S SUPERNATURAL

*Jesus gives us the gift of the Holy Spirit, yet when the Spirit
comes, He is loaded with packages! He desires to release
much more in us and through us than we could ever imagine.
These gifts are given for delivery, not for accumulation. We
receive them to pass them on to others.*
—Jack Hayford[3]

For Johannes Amritzer, childhood wasn't easy by any stretch of
the imagination. His father was a criminal, in and out of prison.
His mother often moved from one abusive boyfriend to the next,
looking for a place to find refuge. Due to this dysfunctional home
life, Johannes bounced from foster home to foster home or was
sent to live for months with a grandma or his aunts and uncles.

Johannes grew up fighting for his life. He turned to alcohol,
sex, and crime to cope and survive. But deep in his spirit he sensed
that he was built for something more. He describes one quiet
moment when he was on a platform in Germany getting ready to
catch a train.

Early one morning, he stood overlooking the train station,
and all he could see were drug addicts, homeless people, and the

prostitutes who were waking up to a new day of misery. At that moment he heard a Voice say to him, "One day, I will use you to reach people just like this." Johannes admits, "Now I know that Voice was the Holy Spirit. But at the time, I had no idea what was happening to me. I thought it might be God talking to me, but I assumed I wasn't worthy of a visitation like that."

Eventually, Johannes's older brother became a Christian. Because of his salvation experience, he did his best to convince his younger brother to give his life to Jesus, as well.

"It was a joke to me," Johannes recounts. "I thought he had lost his mind, and I consistently let him know about it." After refusing many times to attend church, one Sunday Johannes finally showed up.

During that service, his first time at church in a long time, Johannes sensed the same presence he had experienced on the train platform in Germany. By the end of the evening, Johannes had prayed to give his life to Christ.

Shortly after this moment of decision, a youth leader explained to him about the baptism in the Holy Spirit. The leader shared that being baptized in the Holy Spirit would enable God to use Johannes in a supernatural way. So they prayed. Right there, Johannes experienced the outpouring of the Holy Spirit in his life. Out of his lips came the release of power and praise, and he was changed.

No one could have predicted the degree to which Johannes would be used by God. Within a year he was preaching on the streets throughout Sweden, Poland, Germany, and the Czech Republic with Teen Challenge, a youth rebab ministry, and his work was winning the souls of hundreds of skinheads, drug addicts, and other troubled youth for Jesus. The gift of evangelism was obvious in his life, and the Holy Spirit was using him to prove that Jesus is alive and active in the world to rescue us from sin.

As Johannes ministered, supernatural things began to occur. Sick people were healed. Those tormented by demonic spirits were set free. The crowds he ministered to continued to grow as word spread about the young evangelist God was using in supernatural ways.

My friendship with Johannes began in 2002. He and I met when he spoke at a conference I attended in Hampton, Virginia. I sat mesmerized as I listened to him recount how God was doing extraordinary miracles through his ministry overseas. After Johannes had spent time preaching in Sweden and around Europe, God called him to focus his energies on sharing the message of a risen Jesus with people groups that had never heard of Jesus. Mission S.O.S. was born out of this calling. One of my favorite miracle stories took place at one of his festivals in Bulgaria. A crippled Muslim woman was attending the festival. For the first time, she heard how Jesus, who is God in the flesh, had come to earth on a mission to save us. She heard how He died on the cross for her sin and how He rose from the dead. She heard how He was healing people, right there in Bulgaria.

Johannes explained, "She had been crippled for so long that all the muscles in her legs had atrophied. They hung from her body like spaghetti strands, limp, skinny, damaged legs. Her Muslim friends lifted her out of her wheelchair and literally threw her up on stage, demanding: 'Heal her in Jesus's name if you can!'"

"I saw in her eyes the faith to be healed," Johannes continued. "And all of a sudden, I felt a rush of faith within me. The Holy Spirit was shouting to my mind that He was going to heal her body. So before I knew it, I had picked her up, holding her under her arms. I heard myself say, 'I will not let you down until you walk!'"

"As soon as I said it," Johannes confessed, "I thought to myself, 'That's crazy! What are you saying? Now you're really on the spot! What if nothing happens? How long can you hold this woman up in front of this enormous crowd of people?' But I felt the prompting to say it again, so I repeated, 'I will not let you go until you walk.' Then all of a sudden, the woman put her feet on the ground and began to take steps. Her legs were so weak, she couldn't walk without wobbling and without support. But as she stepped out in faith, her legs grew stronger. Right before the eyes of this Islamic crowd, Jesus showed Himself to be alive by healing this woman's broken body."

Over the years of our friendship, I have heard Johannes tell hundreds of such stories. After a few years, I decided to go with him on one of these trips to see some of this for myself. I wasn't disappointed. Deaf people began to hear. Blind eyes were opened. Demon-possessed people cried out as they were set free. It was just like the moments I had read about in the Bible, but now I was living them firsthand. With every trip, I grew more and more hungry to see God's power released in my own life.

"How is this possible?" I asked Johannes early in our friendship.

He replied, "For me, the journey into the supernatural began when I was baptized in the Holy Spirit. None of this would be possible in my life without that first experience." That's what is so amazing about God's plan for His people. The baptism in the Holy Spirit isn't just for the super-Christian who travels the world and speaks to thousands at festivals. The baptism in the Holy Spirit is for *every* believer.

Listen to what Simon Peter said just after his experience with the baptism in the Holy Spirit: *"Repent and be baptized, **every one of you**, in the name of Jesus Christ for the forgiveness of your sins. And you will receive the gift of the Holy Spirit. The promise is for you and for your children and for all who are far off—for all whom the Lord our God will call"* (Acts 2:38–39). This promise is for *you*! It's for your children!

WHAT DOES IT MEAN TO BE BAPTIZED IN THE HOLY SPIRIT?

Jesus challenged His disciples and made them a promise. *"Do not leave Jerusalem, but wait for the gift my Father promised.... For John baptized with water, but in a few days you will be baptized with the Holy Spirit"* (Acts 1:4–5). He was warning them, "Don't try to accomplish the mission without the power. Wait...receive...then take this message into every part of the earth." Then He made the promise: *"You will be baptized with the Holy Spirit."*

To understand this statement, we need to see the comparison. When Jesus referred to John, He was talking about the man known as John the Baptist. John came prior to Jesus. He announced to the people of his day that the kingdom of God was coming to the earth. He challenged his hearers to repent, or turn from, their sinful, selfish ways and surrender to God. Those who heeded his teachings submitted to a symbolic initiation rite called baptism. They were immersed in water, often in the Jordan River.

By being baptized in this way, these people declared that they were leaving their former way of life to follow after God. They went down into the water as sinful, and came up out of the water washed, clean, and new. Baptism was all about beginning something new. It was about being dipped under and enveloped by the waters of the river.

In Greek, the word *baptize* means "to dip under the water" according to dictionary.com. We use a similar word in the English language. The word *capsize* means for a boat to turn over and sink in the water. Every water baptism we see in the Bible involves a person being submerged in a body of water and coming back up completely wet. Jesus was saying to the disciples, "In a few days, you'll be dipped under, totally submerged in, and completely enveloped by the Holy Spirit. And when that happens to you, you'll be filled with the power necessary to prove and witness to My resurrection."

Think about it! Dipped under and enveloped, not by a substance like water, but in a relationship with the Holy Spirit. I haven't talked much about exactly who the Holy Spirit is, but we need to do so now.

WHO IS THE HOLY SPIRIT?

The Holy Spirit is the third person of the Godhead. God is three persons in one being: the Father, the Son, and the Holy Spirit. Just prior to His crucifixion, Jesus introduced the Holy Spirit to the disciples.

Just before Jesus died, He encouraged His disciples with this: *"And I will ask the Father, and he will give you another Helper, to be with you forever, even the Spirit of truth, whom the world cannot receive, because it neither sees him nor knows him. You know him, for he dwells with you and will be in you"* (John 14:16–17 ESV).

The Holy Spirit is just like Jesus. Jesus said the Father *"will give you another Helper."* The word *another* in the Greek implies, "someone who is just like me—who is taking my place" according to *The Intermediate Greek-English Lexicon.* Can you imagine if you could go through life with Jesus walking beside you physically, at every moment? You could consult Him about issues at home or at work. You could ask Him to teach you what to do in a confusing relationship. He would be there to help you when you had a need or didn't know how to pray.

Having the Holy Spirit with you gives you the same benefit. He is the same in essence as Jesus. He is a part of the Trinity just like Jesus. He knows everything God knows, because He is an equal part of the Godhead. You might not be able to see Him, but He is as present with you as anyone ever could be, and even more so. He can advise you, equip you, comfort you, and empower you for life.

The Holy Spirit adds life. Jesus called the Holy Spirit the "Helper" (John 14:16), which in the Greek is *paraclete*. The best way to define this word is by contrast. You understand the word *parasite*. It's a living entity that attaches itself to you to suck the life from you. That's not even fun to think about, and I have experienced it firsthand! Once when I traveled out of the country on a mission trip, I came back with a parasite in my stomach. I was super sick and weak. I felt like the parasite was literally draining the life out of me!

In contrast, we can define a *paraclete* as a living entity that attaches Himself to me to add life onto me. The Holy Spirit strengthens me. He infuses His thoughts into me. He releases His emotions to me: joy, peace, love, patience. He shares His power with me. He gives me what I need at the moment I need it.

The Holy Spirit strengthens me. He infuses His thoughts into me. And he can do the same for you.

The Holy Spirit walks with us through life.

Jesus said the Holy Spirit, *"the Spirit of truth,"* will *"be with you forever."* The Holy Spirit teaches and instructs and reminds us of who Jesus is and what the Bible says. He reinforces the truth of Scripture to us in every way.

Every person who believes in Jesus receives such companionship from the Holy Spirit. He begins to dwell within your life at the moment you confess Christ as your Lord and Savior. In fact, the Holy Spirit is like the "welcoming committee" into God's family. As soon as you pray to receive Christ, the Holy Spirit ignites life on the inside of you. He takes your dead soul and makes it alive. The instant He does that, you know it. Romans 8:16 says, *"The Spirit himself testifies with our spirit that we are God's children."*

So hear this now. The moment you are saved, you receive the Holy Spirit. He lives in you from the moment you become a Christian. And since He lives within you, He immediately begins to give you the capacity to be a better person than you were before. He releases all that He is to you. This moment happened for the original disciples just after Jesus's resurrection. John 20 records the moment when Jesus appeared to the disciples in His resurrected body. *"'Peace be with you! As the Father has sent me, I am sending you.' And with that he breathed on them and said, 'Receive the Holy Spirit'"* (John 20:21–22).

At that moment, Jesus imparted to them the Holy Spirit, just like it happens for us when we pray for salvation. The Holy Spirit took up residence in the disciples' hearts. They received the Holy Spirit as Jesus breathed the Spirit into them.

You might think that would have been enough!

But just a few days later, Jesus told these same disciples, *"Do not leave Jerusalem, but wait for the gift my Father promised.... For John baptized with water, but in a few days you will be baptized with the Holy Spirit"* (Acts 1:4–5).

The disciples had *received* the Holy Spirit in John 20. But they had not yet been *baptized in* the Holy Spirit. Jesus was promising to "dip them under" the Holy Spirit. There is a difference between these two experiences. Having received the Holy Spirit at salvation is the main thing, but if we are to function in the supernatural, we need something more.

WHAT DOES IT MEAN TO BE CLOTHED IN POWER?

This is where it helps to consider different gospel histories. We can hear the words of Jesus from several observers, each account adding value to the overall picture. Luke wrote of the post-resurrection moments that Jesus spent with His disciples. (Remember that Luke penned both the book of Luke and the book of Acts). Here's what Jesus said: *"I am going to send you what my Father has promised; but stay in the city until you have been **clothed with power** from on high"* (Luke 24:49).

The word *clothe* means "to sink into or be plunged into one's clothing; to be arrayed in a garment; to be endued with or placed within." The word *power* is the same word that we saw used in Acts 1. It's the Greek word *dunamis,* which is the root of our English word *dynamite* according to *The Intermediate Greek-English Lexicon.*

Jesus promised to give His disciples some "power clothes" to wear. They were to walk around clothed in and surrounded by the explosive, life-giving power of the Holy Spirit. Everywhere they went and everything they touched would be impacted by these "power clothes." The disciples had already received the Holy Spirit in John 20, when Jesus promised to give them even more. He breathed on them, and then He wanted to clothe them with power.

CAN I REALLY BE "ON FIRE"?

Let's look at another Bible passage. The apostle John recorded the words of John the Baptist when he introduced Jesus to the world:

> *I baptize you with water. But one who is more powerful than I will come* [Jesus], *the straps of whose sandals I am not worthy to untie* [He is so much greater than I am that I am not worthy even to untie His sandals]. *He will baptize you with the Holy Spirit and fire.*   (Luke 3:16)

Let's put it all together:

+ The disciples had already received the Holy Spirit (just like we do when we are saved).

+ Jesus promised them something more.

+ He promised to dip them under or into the Holy Spirit so they would be completely covered by and immersed in His presence.

- When they came out of that baptism experience, they would be clothed with power.

- It would be as though they had been baptized in the fire of God.

I called it "power clothes" above, but I love how Johannes puts it: "When you are baptized in the Holy Spirit, God dresses you in the 'fire clothes' of Jesus." In other words, you walk around wearing the fiery power of God on your life. And just as Jesus performed supernatural acts through the power of the Holy Spirit, so you can expect to see the supernatural through that same Holy Spirit power. Even though Jesus went to heaven, so He is no longer present physically, He left behind His fire clothes for every believer to wear, bestowing His power on us.

There's a great story in 2 Kings about the powerful old prophet Elijah and his spiritual son, Elisha. God used Elijah to do amazing miracles. This prophet experienced incredible answers to his prayers. Once, God answered his prayer and raised a boy back to life who had died. When God took Elijah to heaven, the prophet left behind his mantle or outer cloak for the younger man Elisha to wear. The cloak was filled with the sweat and aroma of Elijah.

> [Elisha] *took the cloak that had fallen from Elijah and struck the water* [of the Jordan River] *with it. "Where now is the* LORD, *the God of Elijah?" he asked. When he struck the water, it divided to the right and to the left, and he crossed over. The company of the prophets* [bystanders] *from Jericho, who were watching, said, "The spirit of Elijah is resting on Elisha."*   (2 Kings 2:14–15)

Can you see the parallels here? As Elijah left his mantle for Elisha, so Jesus left behind His "mantle" for us. He wants us to carry the same Spirit upon us that was upon Him. He wants to clothe us in power. He wants to baptize us in the Holy Spirit and in fire. He wants us to put on His fire clothes and walk around as instruments of Holy Spirit explosiveness.

Do you long for this?

Do you want the Father to clothe you in power? Do you want to wear the fire clothes of Jesus?

As we are baptized in the Holy Spirit, we can enter the challenging places of life and say, "Where now is the power of Jesus?" And as we step out in faith to be used by God, He will release miracles through us to the world.

One of my great moments as a father happened a few years ago. My oldest son, David, felt a call into the ministry. He gave his life to Christ at a young age, and when he was a teen, he was baptized in the Holy Spirit. When he graduated from high school, he went on a mission trip to Nicaragua where he prayed for the sick during the meetings.

I'll never forget his report of that trip. "Dad, I prayed for a man who was blind. His eyes were all cloudy. And as I prayed in the name of Jesus, I could see the cloudiness disappear. He started waving his arms, and we both knew what had happened: He could see!" Then David added, "It was totally awesome!"

Once you have had an experience like that, you will never view the Christian life in the same way. No longer is it a philosophy of life or a set of moral teachings. No longer is being a Christian just about going to church and trying to be a good person. When you are baptized in the Holy Spirit and you step out to see the power of God released through your life, the Christian life becomes an adventure of following a risen Jesus and showing the world that He is alive and still doing miracles in the world today.

CHAPTER THREE DISCUSSION QUESTIONS

1. Have you ever worn special equipment or a uniform for a job or a sport? If so, why was it necessary to be clothed like that?

2. Read Luke 24:49. How would you explain this promise to someone?

3. If we really believed we were "clothed" in the power of God, how would we act and react in life?

4. Read 2 Kings 2:14. Elisha picked up the miraculous cloak or mantle of Elijah and then acted in faith. What would it mean for you to take hold of the "mantle" or fire clothes of Jesus by the power of the Holy Spirit?

FOUR

IT'S VERBAL

*If it is in the Bible, it is so. It's not even to be prayed about.
It's to be received and acted upon. Inactivity is a robber
which steals blessings. Increase comes by action,
by using what we have and know. Your life must be one
of going on from faith to faith.*
—Smith Wigglesworth[4]

To be honest, I had some bad experiences as the son of a Pentecostal minister.

I was baptized in the Holy Spirit on October 20, 1980. I'll never forget it, but not just because it was an experience that changed my life. I'll never forget it because it was the culmination of a five-month season where I questioned everything about this experience in general.

Just a few months prior, I had attended a youth camp. One evening, the message was about the experience that Jesus called being baptized in the Holy Spirit. At the conclusion of the message, the speaker called us forward if we wanted to be filled with the Holy Spirit. Well, I was ready. I couldn't wait for the moment to arrive. The message had filled me with such vision and hunger for the presence and power of God that I ran to the front as soon as they gave us the opportunity.

I understood what the Bible taught about this moment. In just about every case in the book of Acts when people were baptized in the Holy Spirit, they responded to His presence by declaring their praise out loud.

> *All of them were filled with the Holy Spirit and began to speak in other tongues as the Spirit enabled them.*   (Acts 2:4)

> *The Holy Spirit came on all who heard the message. The [Jewish] believers who had come with Peter were astonished that the gift of the Holy Spirit had been poured out even on the Gentiles [non-Jews]. For they heard them speaking in tongues and praising God.*   (Acts 10:44–46)

> *When Paul placed his hands on them, the Holy Spirit came on them, and they spoke in tongues and prophesied.*
>   (Acts 19:6)

When I went to the front to receive the baptism in the Holy Spirit, I fully expected to speak in tongues. The speaker that evening had done a great job of painting the picture of what happened to those who experienced the Holy Spirit in the book of Acts. I was ready, and so were those who were praying for me.

I guess it shows that I was loved, but there were way too many people converged to pray for me that night. It was a hot summer evening, and about fifteen of my friends and youth leaders were gathered around me. Most of them placed a hand on my head, or shoulder, or arm. The Bible talks about laying hands on people in prayer, and these good friends were reaching out to encourage me. Some were swaying as they prayed, so this large crowd of people (with me in the center) began to sway back and forth like the waves of the ocean. Many of them were praying out loud; some were shouting encouragements.

"Receive! In Jesus's name! Now speak it out! Release the gift! Be filled! Be filled!"

I sometimes joke that someone was saying, "Hold on, hold on!" and another was saying, "Let go, let go!" I'm not sure if that's true or not, but I can tell you that I was thoroughly confused, frustrated, and overwhelmed by the expectation for me to perform some spiritual feat on cue. It was religious pandemonium. And it went on and on for what seemed like hours (although it was probably only about fifteen minutes).

Finally, I got the courage to break out of the circle of expectation. I retreated to the front row and sat with my head in my hands, hoping people would just leave me alone to think for a minute. Some friends came over to sit next to me and kept praying. I had to ask them to stop, and explained that I just needed a few minutes to pray on my own. They respected that, but I could tell they were disappointed. They desperately wanted me to experience a breakthrough in this area, and nothing seemed to happen visibly.

My reaction to that experience was to question everything. My thoughts went something like this:

+ Is something wrong with me? Do I have sin in my life, and that's why I couldn't speak in tongues?

+ Maybe everyone is just crazy. How can this be from God?

+ What in the world is this "speaking in tongues" thing anyway? Is it really in the Bible?

+ Is speaking in tongues really necessary? Why do they make such a big deal out of it? It just seems weird to me!

+ What does speaking in tongues have to do with the baptism in the Holy Spirit? Can't I just be filled with the Spirit without all this other stuff?

⁘ I'm more of a private person, so can't I experience this in my own way? Do I really have to declare anything out loud to be baptized in the Holy Spirit?

For five months, I wrestled through these questions. I asked my dad to sit down with me, and I interrogated him on what the Bible teaches. He calmly answered every one of my questions from the Bible. I had to admit that being filled with the Spirit was in there. There was no denying the verses listed in the book of Acts and in other books like 1 Corinthians. But I still wasn't ready to deal with the disappointment I felt from that night at youth camp. I decided just to put the whole idea on the shelf for a while...but God wouldn't allow it. Every place I went, people were talking about it.

I showed up at church, and the speaker selected a passage of Scripture for his text that dealt with the baptism in the Holy Spirit. A few days later, I attended a youth small group, and the students leading the meeting brought up the topic and shared their testimonies about being filled with the Spirit. Even when I turned on a Christian radio station, someone was preaching about it. Dare I say it was kind of spooky?

Finally, I had my moment of breakthrough in my living room one night after our youth small group had met and once again the baptism in the Holy Spirit had been the topic of discussion.

Out of frustration, I said to one of my friends, "I give up! I know God wants me to experience the baptism in the Holy Spirit, but I just don't think it will ever happen for me."

My friend gently and quietly challenged me, "Let's pray right now."

As we prayed, just the two of us in that quiet room, I began to feel something happen within me. It was that warm sensation in my chest that I often felt when I was in church or in a season of worship. It grew stronger and stronger as I verbalized praise to God.

Then my friend said to me, "God is all over you! I can sense that He's baptizing you in the Holy Spirit at this moment. Now, what you need to do is tune in to what He says to you. When you hear a syllable in your spirit that you don't recognize in English, just speak it out loud. That's what speaking in tongues is. It is speaking in a language that God supernaturally gives to you. So just say what you hear in your heart."

Just like that, I spoke out in a spiritual language. As I did, I felt that rush of the river of the Holy Spirit flowing from within me. It was amazing. I kept on praying out loud what the Holy Spirit gave me to say. As I did this, His presence flooded my being over and over again. An hour in prayer this way felt like just a few minutes.

I have never been the same since that night! The baptism in the Holy Spirit is a promise that is given to all who show up for it.

I realize that you may have some of the same questions I wrestled through. Just like my father did, I want to calmly and biblically address these questions one at a time. My dad sat with me at the kitchen table. We both pulled out our Bibles, and he took me through passage after passage to address my objections. Let's sit together for a moment and do the same.

QUESTION 1: IS SOMETHING WRONG WITH ME? DO I HAVE SIN IN MY LIFE AND THAT'S WHY I CAN'T SPEAK IN TONGUES?

It is such a deflating feeling to believe that God has singled you out as unworthy. That was the bottom line of how I felt: rejected, unworthy, exposed, and judged before the entire world and found wanting. No one should ever feel this way. Often, where this experience is concerned, well-meaning people put a huge amount of pressure on those seeking to be baptized in the Holy Spirit. The result is that when people fail to speak in tongues, they feel like something is wrong with them or wrong with the entire idea of Holy Spirit baptism.

First of all, we need to understand that the baptism in the Holy Spirit is a *gift*. This is how Jesus described the experience to the disciples. *"Do not leave Jerusalem, but wait for the **gift** my Father promised"* (Acts 1:4). The word used here in the Greek is *epaggelia*, which means "to announce the fulfillment of a promised good thing to be given" according to Strong's Concordance.

The baptism in the Holy Spirit is a promise that is given to all who ask for it. It isn't something we earn by being worthy. It's something we obtain simply by showing up to receive what God has promised to give us.

I'm writing this chapter of the book in a coffee shop. Earlier today, I received an email from this shop announcing that if I showed up today, I would receive a free specialty drink because I had a birthday last month. The coffee shop gave me an *epaggelia* (a declared promise of a good thing to be given). When I showed up to receive my free drink, I wasn't thinking about whether or not I was worthy to obtain this grande cappuccino. I didn't do any self-examination before I made the request of the barista. I just asked to receive what the shop had promised me.

In a similar way, the Father promises to give the Holy Spirit to anyone who asks. It's a gift that He gives by grace. None of us will ever deserve this gift, but God wants to give the Holy Spirit to *all* those who ask. In another place, Jesus said, *"If you then, though you are evil, know how to give good gifts to your children, how much more will your Father in heaven give the Holy Spirit to those who ask him!"* (Luke 11:13).

First, the baptism in the Holy Spirit is a *gift* that is promised by the Father; we cannot earn it. Second, the baptism in the Holy Spirit is a *grant* that is conveyed by God so that we can begin to operate according to His purpose.

When I went to college, I applied to several organizations to receive a grant: funds conveyed to me to pay for my studies. Several of these organizations approved me and released a grant to me so I could afford to do what I wouldn't have been able to do otherwise. This is what the Father wants for you and me. He wants to convey the Holy Spirit on us as a grant, giving us the capacity to be a witness for the resurrected Jesus, which we can't accomplish without His help.

I fought with feelings of unworthiness when I wasn't able to speak in tongues right away, but you don't have to be worthy to receive this gift or to be given this grant. You just need to show up and ask for it. God won't reject you and He won't judge you as inferior or lacking. He won't single you out as someone who is a disappointment to Him. He won't expose you as a fraud or a failure. He wants to give you what He promised. I can say from personal experience that it's fruitless to spend a lot of time grieving over your own unworthiness, and doing so places the emphasis on the wrong thing entirely.

Yes, if you look close enough at my life, you'll find plenty of reasons why God should just leave me and reject me. I fail. I'm a sinner. I fall short of perfection. My life is often selfish and sinful.

But God didn't save me because I was worthy. He saved me because He loved me. He loves me more than I can understand, and He isn't going to change His mind about that fact. Not only does He love me, He accepts me and wants to do amazing things in my life.

In the same way, the Father wants to give me the Holy Spirit in greater measure just because He has chosen to do that for me. I'm His child; He's my Father. He knows how to give His kids His best gifts. So if I ask for the outpouring of the Holy Spirit in my life, He has promised to give it to me. I don't have to earn it. I don't have to prove that I'm worthy of it. All I can do is receive it.

QUESTION 2: MAYBE EVERYONE IS JUST CRAZY. HOW CAN THIS BE FROM GOD?

This is often the response I hear to the very idea of speaking in tongues. It just sounds odd, doesn't it? Maybe it's just me, but the first time I heard of this, I thought, "What? Speaking in a language you have never studied? Impossible! Weird! Spooky!"

Then I heard a woman speaking in tongues in church. I think I was seven or eight years old. She was seated in the pew just behind me, praying in a very high-pitched tone, and it startled me. All of a sudden, she closed her eyes, started to cry, and belted out a prayer in a language that sounded something like Chinese to me. It freaked me out! I thought to myself, "I will do a lot of things in life, but I will never do that!"

Later, as I read the Bible for myself, I discovered this is something real. It's biblical. Over centuries, millions of people have practiced it. The apostle Paul said, *"I thank God that I speak in tongues more than all of you"* (1 Corinthians 14:18). He was writing to the Corinthian church, which was well-known for their use and pursuit of spiritual gifts. Obviously, for Paul, this was a regular and normal experience.

Once I had prayed in tongues, I understood that this experience isn't spooky at all. I didn't have to stop being the quiet, introverted, private person that I am to pray in a spiritual language. I have never prayed in a loud, high-pitched tone like that woman who scared me when I was seven. My nature isn't to be overly emotional, even when God is working in my life. I haven't had to become loud or emotional to experience the Holy Spirit's work in my life. The great thing is, people who are naturally loud and emotional don't have to be like me. They can be who they are and respond to God according to their own personality.

QUESTION 3: WHAT IN THE WORLD IS THIS "SPEAKING IN TONGUES" THING, ANYWAY?

"Speaking in tongues" is a way to describe "speaking in another language." In the book of Revelation, heaven is described as a place where every tribe and "tongue" will be present. *"After these things I looked, and behold, a great multitude which no one could number, of all nations, tribes, peoples, and tongues, standing before the throne and before the Lamb"* (Revelation 7:9 NKJV). The word *"tongues"* is used to describe various language groups. What makes the biblical experience of speaking in tongues unique is that it's a supernatural act, a linguistic miracle, by which we speak out in a language we have never studied and don't naturally understand.

The first time this occurred in history is recorded in Acts 2. The people who had gathered there heard others speaking "in tongues" and knew that a miracle was happening.

> *Now there were staying in Jerusalem God-fearing Jews from every nation.... When they heard this sound, a crowd came together in bewilderment, because each one heard their own language being spoken. Utterly amazed, they asked, "Aren't all these who are speaking Galileans? Then how is it that each of us hears them in our native language?"* (Acts 2:5–8)

As we participate in this "language miracle," God does several things:

HE REVEALS JESUS TO THOSE WHO HEAR.

When the believers were first baptized in the Holy Spirit, the people around them said, *"'We hear them declaring the wonders of God in our own tongues!' Amazed and perplexed, they asked one another, 'What does this mean?'"* (Acts 2:11–12).

As you can imagine, this miracle of language was pretty convincing. The people knew such a thing could only happen if God were at work. Thousands gathered to hear Simon Peter speak because they had witnessed this language miracle. Speaking in tongues is just one of the many supernatural things that God wants to do in our lives.

My wife's grandparents Lewie and Evelyn Spencer were missionaries in Costa Rica back in the 1930s. They wanted to take the message of Jesus to tribes of people who had never heard about Him. Their only mode of transportation to these remote areas was on the back of a mule. They would travel for days, over high mountains, to reach these tribes and share the good news of salvation.

On one occasion, they encountered a tribe that was completely unfamiliar to them. None of their interpreters knew the dialect. The Spencers tried to communicate, but nothing seemed to work, so they stopped to pray. They gathered in a circle and prayed for God to help them. As they prayed, my wife's grandparents began to speak in tongues.

As soon as they started praying that way, the members of the tribe became animated. They began to jump up and down and wave their arms. It was obvious that something significant was happening. Within a few hours, they found an interpreter, and he helped the Spencers communicate with the tribe.

As soon as they started to converse, one of the tribe members asked, "How did you come to learn our language? When you gathered in that circle and started talking to the sky, one of you started telling us that God had sent you to us with some good news. How do you know our language?"

When the Spencers explained that God had performed a language miracle through them and that He had done this because He loved the people, the entire tribe was ready to hear the message about Jesus Christ.

HE USES THIS TO HELP US PRAY MORE EFFECTIVELY.

Most often, speaking in tongues is used privately and in prayer. The Holy Spirit prompts us to pray in a special prayer language. We don't know how to pray as well as the Holy Spirit does, so He helps us pray better.

Romans 8:26–27 says, *"In the same way, the Spirit helps us in our weakness. We do not know what we ought to pray for, but the Spirit himself intercedes for us through wordless groans. And he who searches our hearts knows the mind of the Spirit, because the Spirit intercedes for God's people in accordance with the will of God."*

First Corinthians 14:2 adds, *"For anyone who speaks in a tongue **does not speak to people but to God**. Indeed, no one understands them; they utter mysteries by the Spirit."*

QUESTION 4: IS SPEAKING IN TONGUES REALLY NECESSARY?

Many people ask, "Do I have to speak in tongues to be baptized in the Holy Spirit?" I like to respond with the same explanation my father gave to me, "It's not that you *have* to speak in tongues; it's that you *get* to speak in tongues." You have the opportunity to allow the Holy Spirit to be released through you as you pray. The Spirit of God is praying through you as He is praying for you and for those in your world. That's amazing!

Every time people were baptized in the Holy Spirit in the book of Acts, they prayed aloud in a supernatural way. When the Holy Spirit comes upon you, He gives you power to prove that Jesus is alive. The baptism in the Holy Spirit is the first step into a supernatural life. Not only does God want to do this language miracle in you, He wants to use you to see many powerful and miraculous things happen in the name of Jesus.

Remember, the goal of the baptism in the Holy Spirit is not for you to speak in tongues. Did you hear that? Speaking in tongues is *not* the goal. The goal of the baptism in the Holy Spirit is to give you power to prove that Jesus is alive. The baptism in the Holy Spirit is a gift that releases the power of God into and through your life. Speaking in another language is just the first miracle that God wants to do through you. It certainly isn't the last miracle He will do through you. He has so much more planned for you!

Sometimes, people have approached the baptism in the Holy Spirit as the completion of something. They pray for it. They receive it. They experience the first miracle of praying in a spiritual language, but that's the finale for them. They stop seeking more of God's power. They stop expecting more miracles to be released into their lives. What a shame. This experience was never designed to be an end in and of itself; it was always designed to be the beginning of a powerful spiritual life.

It's the starting point for living out a supernatural life.

QUESTION 5: WHAT DOES SPEAKING IN TONGUES HAVE TO DO WITH THE BAPTISM IN THE HOLY SPIRIT? CAN'T I JUST BE FILLED WITH THE SPIRIT WITHOUT ALL THIS OTHER STUFF?

The real question is this: Why do you want to be baptized in the Holy Spirit? Do you just want to be able to say that it happened for you? Do you want to cross it off the list of things you have experienced in life? Do you just want to feel better about yourself, knowing that you have attained a certain spiritual plateau and don't need anything more?

Or are you seeking to live a supernatural life? Do you desire to be a powerful witness of the resurrection of Jesus? Do you want to be a vessel Jesus can use to deliver His miracles to broken and needy people? Are you hungry to know the full release of the river of the Holy Spirit in your life? Do you want to feel the rush of His presence, purpose, and power unleashed through you?

If you want a supernatural life, then you need to think of speaking in tongues as the first miracle that He will do through you.

Why is this the first? Why can't He do other miracles with you first? Why does it have to be this?

The Bible gives a list of nine miraculous ways that God uses believers. It's found in 1 Corinthians 12 and it involves things like gifts of healing, word of wisdom, words of knowledge, prophecy, and faith. The Spirit of God distributes these gifts to each believer as He determines for the common good of the entire body of Christ.

Yet He begins with the baptism in the Holy Spirit and the linguistic miracle of speaking in tongues for several reasons:

+ *It's personal.* No one else has to be there. It's just you and the Holy Spirit. All you have to do to see this miracle is to speak out the words that He gives you to say.

+ *It's a partnership.* Since speaking in tongues involves just you and the Holy Spirit, you practice a partnership with the Holy Spirit as you pray in your spiritual language. Every time you pray in tongues, you are practicing what it is to operate in the supernatural. You are tuning in to His voice. You are speaking out what you have heard in the Spirit. These are all skills you will need when He uses you in a public fashion.

+ *It's powerful.* Every time you speak in tongues, the strength of the Holy Spirit is released within you. This gives power to your inner being. Paul described it like this, *"Anyone who speaks in a tongue edifies* [builds up and adds strength to] *themselves"* (1 Corinthians 14:4).

This practice of praying in the Spirit becomes a gateway to a supernatural life. The Holy Spirit is released in your inner being, and His power comes out through your lips before it comes out in your life.

CHAPTER FOUR DISCUSSION QUESTIONS

1. When you first heard of the practice of speaking in tongues, what was your reaction?

2. Have you ever felt undue pressure to do something spiritually that perhaps you weren't ready to do? What effect did that have on you?

3. What is the right motive to pursue any significant experience with God? What are some wrong motives?

4. Read Romans 8:26–28. What is the role of the Holy Spirit in your prayer life and in fulfilling God's purpose for your life?

5. What next steps are you going to take to give the Holy Spirit a more active role in the way you pray?

FIVE
IT'S PRAYERFUL

In the same way, the Spirit helps us in our weakness.
We do not know what we ought to pray for, but the Spirit
himself intercedes for us through wordless groans.
And he who searches our hearts knows the mind of the
Spirit, because the Spirit intercedes for God's people in
accordance with the will of God.
—Romans 8:26–27

A little over a decade ago, a man named Bashar lived with his family in Iraq. As the atmosphere in that nation grew more dangerous, he knew it was time to move his family out of harm's way. He found a place for his wife and kids to stay in Syria. After getting them settled, Bashar made his way to Sweden, where he could apply for refugee status, attempt to get a job, and prepare to bring his family with him to Sweden.

Shortly after arriving in Sweden, Bashar met Johannes Amritzer on a subway train. Johannes shared the message of Christ with Bashar and invited him to attend church in Stockholm. Before long, Bashar made the decision to give his life to Christ. He was baptized in water and a while later was baptized in the Holy Spirit.

Every day Bashar grew in his faith. Every day he prayed for his wife and kids, who were living thousands of miles away. Johannes had taught him the value of praying in tongues, and Bashar practiced this on a regular basis. When he entered his prayer time, he began by praying in his native language of Arabic. Then, as he worshipped God, he would speak out the syllables he felt the Holy Spirit inspired him to say.

Soon this practice of praying in the Spirit became comfortable to him. He was tuning in to the Holy Spirit's operation within his heart. He was speaking out in faith what he sensed the Holy Spirit prompted within. As he did this, he felt stronger and perceived himself to be operating in the flow of the Holy Spirit's work within him.

One day, Bashar received a call from his wife. Life was becoming increasingly dangerous in Syria, so she wanted to take the children back across the border into Iraq. She felt that returning there to live with friends, in the neighborhood she knew best, would be the safest option. Bashar asked her to remain where she was until he'd had the chance to think and pray about this idea.

Bashar recounts, "Something inside of me didn't feel right about the move. So I began to pour out my heart to God in prayer. In Farsi, I prayed for God to give me direction and to protect my family. But somehow, that didn't seem to be enough. So I began to pray in my spiritual language." Throughout the day, Bashar prayed in the Spirit for his wife and children and whether they should leave Syria and return to Iraq.

Suddenly, God spoke to him clearly as he prayed in tongues. A strong inner sense of warning said, "Do not let your wife go back to Iraq." As Bashar continued to pray, the inner impression grew stronger and stronger. He picked up the phone and called his wife. "I feel that you must not leave Syria," he told her. "You must stay where you are."

She responded, "But I don't feel safe here. I have already made calls and arranged for us to go, and we are preparing to leave right now."

Bashar insisted urgently, "I am your husband, and you and the children mean everything to me. I must insist that you stay in Syria. Please don't go to Iraq under any circumstance."

Then he explained to her what had happened as he prayed. He told her that the Holy Spirit had warned him about the dangers in Iraq. Even though it seemed a logical move to leave Syria, God had said his wife was to stay there. When she heard his explanation, she agreed to remain where she was for at least a few more weeks.

Two days later, a suicide bomber detonated an explosive in the neighborhood in Iraq where Bashar's family would have been staying. The room in the apartment building his family would have been sleeping in was completely destroyed. Had his wife crossed the border and returned to Iraq, she and the children would have died in that explosion.

When I first met Bashar, in Sweden, he recounted this story to me. Then he added, "Pastor, you must teach everyone you know about the baptism in the Holy Spirit. I pray in tongues all the time. Praying in the Spirit saved my family. It's the best gift I have ever received."

In the previous chapter, we discussed the initial miracle that occurs when we are baptized in the Holy Spirit. We begin to speak out (pray) in a language we have never studied or learned. This is a language miracle. We call this "praying in tongues," or "praying in the Spirit." I have also used the phrase "praying in my spiritual language." The Bible records two uses for this language miracle:

Prayer: The primary purpose is a private and personal one. Most often, the use of a spiritual language is to assist us to pray as the Holy Spirit prays through us. We will discuss this use of the language miracle throughout the rest of this chapter.

Proclamation: The second purpose is a public one. The book of 1 Corinthians, chapters 12 and 14, mentions two spiritual gifts that almost always work together in a public setting: tongues and the interpretation of tongues.

> *Tongues, then, are a sign, not for believers but for unbelievers.*   (1 Corinthians 14:22)

> *If anyone speaks in a tongue, two—or at the most three—should speak, one at a time, and someone must interpret. If there is no interpreter, the speaker should keep quiet in the church and speak to himself and to God.*
> (1 Corinthians 14:27–28)

Here Paul gave instructions to the church at Corinth as to how spiritual gifts should operate in their public gatherings. He outlined the purpose for the combination of tongues and interpretation. Tongues served as a "sign" for unbelievers. How so? It is a bilingual miracle. If a person entered the public service and heard someone speak supernaturally in the hearer's native language, and then heard another person supernaturally interpret that message, that would be a pretty convincing sign that God was at work!

But the governing rules are these: Speaking in tongues has no value in a public service unless it is accompanied by an interpretation and therefore is used as a sign to a specific unbeliever that God is at work. Notice what Paul says in verse 28. If no interpreter is present, the one speaking in tongues should keep quiet in the church (the public place of use) and should speak only to himself and to God (using tongues in prayer).

We see that there are two uses for the spiritual language: one is public, and one is private. One use is for proclamation; the other use is for private prayer. Many believers will never use tongues publicly to proclaim a message that will be supernaturally interpreted.

But everyone can expect to use tongues personally and in prayer. Notice how the apostle Paul described his own experience:

> I thank God that I speak in tongues more than all of you [privately and in prayer]. But in the church [publicly and to proclaim] I would rather speak five intelligible words to instruct others than ten thousand words in a tongue.
> (1 Corinthians 14:18–19)

What are the benefits of speaking in tongues in your personal prayer life?

INTERCESSION

The word *intercession* means "pleading or advocating on behalf of another." This is what the Holy Spirit does for us when we pray in our spiritual language. He uses our lips and our voices to pray accurately, powerfully, and effectively to God about situations of great importance. The Holy Spirit interceded through Bashar for his family members who were in grave danger.

> In the same way, the Spirit helps us in our weakness. We do not know what we ought to pray for, but the Spirit himself intercedes for us through wordless groans. And he who searches our hearts knows the mind of the Spirit, because the Spirit intercedes for God's people in accordance with the will of God. (Romans 8:26–27)

+ *Our prayers need help.* Often, we don't know what to pray for. Some situations are so complicated that we don't even know where to begin. The Spirit helps us in our weakness and intercedes through us. He knows exactly what we need to pray.

+ *Our prayers lack accuracy.* When we pray, we are uncertain as to what God's will is in specific situations. But the "*Spirit intercedes...in accordance with the will of God."* He knows exactly what God's will is.

+ *Our prayers require expression.* Often words simply aren't enough. At times, we feel so burdened in our spirits that saying words into the air seems incomplete. But the Spirit helps us carry that inner burden to the Lord. The Holy Spirit groans along with us until our need has been carried into the heavens and deposited in the hands of God.

As a young boy, I remember hearing the phrase "praying through." Someone would say, "I need to pray through about this." They meant, "I need to pray in the Spirit until the burden I feel in my spirit lifts off me." When we feel a heaviness in our spirits about something, it often feels like a weight on our chest. Praying in the Spirit is a way of gradually pushing that weight off ourselves and onto the shoulders of the Lord.

EDIFICATION

Edification is defined by 1 Corinthians 14:3 as "the act of uplifting, strengthening, and inwardly benefiting." The passage in 1 Corinthians 14 provides so much insight into this practice of praying in the Spirit. One of the benefits listed is personal edification. Every time I pray in the Spirit, I feel uplifted and strengthened in my spirit. Let's break down the specifics in these verses:

+ Speaking in tongues helps us talk to God.

For anyone who speaks in a tongue does not speak to people but to God.   (1 Corinthians 14:2)

+ When I speak in tongues, I don't understand what I'm saying. I let the Holy Spirit talk to God through me directly to the Father.

Indeed, no one understands them [the person speaking in tongues]; *they utter mysteries by the Spirit.*

(1 Corinthians 14:2)

+ Prophecy is the public gift that has the most value because it's a clear way of speaking understandable words that edify those who hear them. Prophecy strengthens, encourages, and comforts others.

But the one who prophesies speaks to people for their strengthening, encouraging and comfort. (1 Corinthians 14:3)

+ When I speak in tongues, I edify myself. I'm speaking in a way that also strengthens, encourages, and comforts my own soul.

Anyone who speaks in a tongue edifies themselves, but the one who prophesies edifies the church. (1 Corinthians 14:4)

+ Everyone would benefit by praying in tongues.

I would like every one of you to speak in tongues.

(1 Corinthians 14:5)

A few years ago, my dear friend Bruce Edwards was in a swimming accident off the coast of Delaware. Bruce was knocked off his feet by a wave, hit the ocean floor with his head, and was instantly paralyzed. By the time he reached the hospital, after being life-flighted from the coast, his brain had been severely impaired. For ten days, Bruce was in the ICU in a hospital in Philadelphia. My wife and I made the drive across Pennsylvania at least four times during that ten-day period. Not only was Bruce a close friend of almost thirty years, he was a pastor on my staff.

Many times during those difficult days, I didn't know what or how to pray. I felt shocked, confused, depleted, and empty. But I knew I needed to provide strength and presence to Bruce's family during this season as they stood by his bedside during those critical moments. So I prayed in the Spirit.

There are two practices that have a similar effect on my soul. I feel stronger inside when I worship. I feel stronger inside when I pray in tongues. Worship lifts my spirit because I invite and step into the presence of God. Praying in tongues is a release to my spirit because this lifts the weight on my heart and deposits it into the care of God. It provides peace and release. As I traveled back and forth to the hospital, I spent the time worshipping and praying in tongues. This made me stronger in every way.

When I prayed in the Spirit during those moments in the ICU, I felt the Holy Spirit release everything I needed. He gave me peace that surpassed my understanding, strength to minister to the family, and the ability to access the resources of His grace in those moments of tremendous need.

CONFRONTATION

Confrontation is the act of opposing groups clashing with one another and challenging each other. The Bible declares that we are in a place of constant confrontation with the forces of darkness. Ephesians 6:10–13 challenges us: *"Be strong in the Lord and in his mighty power…so that you can take your stand against the devil's schemes. For our struggle is not against flesh and blood, but against the rulers, against the authorities, against the powers of this dark world and against the spiritual forces of evil in the heavenly realms."*

Following this challenge is a list of ways we need to prepare ourselves for this ongoing and constant fight. It involves wearing spiritual armor much like a gladiator or Roman soldier would have worn: a helmet, a breastplate, a belt, shoes/shin guards, a sword, and a shield. The sword is compared to how we use God's Word. It's sharp and cuts through the lies and deceptions of the devil and his dark attempts to destroy us.

*In addition to all this, take up the shield of faith with which you can extinguish all the flaming arrows of the evil one. Take the helmet of salvation and the sword of the Spirit, which is the word of God. And **pray in the spirit on all occasions** with all kinds of prayers and requests. With this in mind, be alert and keep on praying for all the Lord's people.*

(Ephesians 6:16–18)

Praying as prompted by the Holy Spirit is an offensive weapon in spiritual warfare. The best illustration of the experience of spiritual warfare is the feel of the current when you walk out into the ocean. Every few steps, a wave crashes against your body. You have to stand strong to keep from being pushed over. The current not only tries to push you back, it tends to drag you down the shore. If you aren't careful, the ocean current will pull you when you think you are standing still. You have to pay attention constantly to how the push of the waters is affecting you. As we pray in our spiritual language, we are not only pushing the weight off our spirits, we are also pushing against the current of darkness.

The devil sends a spiritual current against your life every day. If you aren't aware, it can knock you over. If you aren't vigilant, it can carry you to a place you don't want to go. If you want to go somewhere positive with your life, you have to push intentionally against the current to gain new ground toward a better place.

Praying in the Spirit helps us push against that current. Actually, praying in the Spirit creates a countercurrent. The power of the Holy Spirit releases a new wave within you that is headed in the opposite direction of the devil. God begins to push against the darkness through you. The Holy Spirit is released like the blowing of a new wind that will carry you over the rough waters and into a place where you are sailing over the attacks against your life.

FORTIFICATION

Fortification has to do with making something stronger by rooting it deeply into a relationship with something or someone else. When we pray in the Holy Spirit, we are connected and established in our relationship with Christ. *"But you, dear friends, by building yourself up in your most holy faith and **praying in the Holy Spirit,** keep yourself in God's love as you wait for the mercy of our Lord Jesus Christ to bring you to eternal life"* (Jude 20–21).

The Holy Spirit establishes us in God's love. He reveals the fact that God never stops loving us, no matter what. When we pray in the Spirit, the Holy Spirit reminds us that we are adopted and accepted by God.

The Holy Spirit reminds us of truth. Jesus said in John 16:13, *"When he, the Spirit of truth, comes, he will guide you into all the truth."* Praying in the Spirit affirms, confirms, and unlocks the truths in the Scripture.

The Holy Spirit strengthens our faith. As we pray in the Spirit, our capacity to believe what God has promised increases. The Holy Spirit possesses all the faith and all the power that we need. As He operates within us, more and more of what He has becomes available to us.

REVELATION

Revelation is defined as "making something evident" or "disclosing that which is hidden." The entire next chapter is devoted to this benefit of praying in the Spirit. Many times we need to know something that is hidden from us. God knows, but we don't know. As we pray in tongues, the Holy Spirit reveals things we could never know otherwise.

Bashar experienced a revelation from God. As he prayed in the Holy Spirit, God impressed on his mind that danger lurked in Iraq, where his family wanted to go. Logically, it seemed as if traveling back there would be less dangerous than to remain where they were staying in Syria. But the Holy Spirit knew the facts. He knew that on a particular day, at a specific time, an explosion would destroy the very apartment where Bashar's wife and family would have been, had they returned. This revelation from the Holy Spirit preserved their lives.

This is the kind of experience we can expect when we are baptized in the Holy Spirit. The next chapter is all about just how much God can reveal into your life.

CHAPTER FIVE DISCUSSION QUESTIONS

1. Have you ever participated in an activity that required accuracy—for example, firing a bow and arrow or throwing darts? What are some of the keys to accuracy?

2. Why is the Holy Spirit more accurate than we are when it comes to praying according to the will of God?

3. Research tells us that there is an aftereffect to exercise. Endorphins are released into your system after a workout, giving you a rush of energy and emotion. They call this a "runner's high." In a similar way, praying in the Holy Spirit edifies your inner spirit. How does that work, in your opinion?

4. Have you ever felt that God spoke by the Holy Spirit into your life? Can you describe how that worked and what it was like?

5. What can you do this week to position yourself to hear from God in a greater way?

SIX
IT'S REVELATIONAL

When we pray in the Spirit, the Bible says that we pray
mysteries with our spirit unto God. Usually we don't know
what we are praying about, but the Spirit knows and prays
for us according to God's will. And God is a reciprocal God.
As we pray mysteries with our spirit, the pipeline of heaven is
open, and God reveals mysteries back to us as well.
—Ron Johnson, Pastor, One Church, Orlando, Florida

In October of 2012, Ron Johnson traveled from his home in Orlando, Florida, to attend a pastors' roundtable in Huntsville, Alabama. All the participants checked into the hotel and made their way down to dinner. After the first day of meetings was over, Ron began to feel a deep uneasiness in his spirit. Something wasn't right.

He retreated to his room and began to pray in the Spirit, seeking God for the reason why he felt so disturbed. First Corinthians 12 describes various expressions or manifestations of the Holy Spirit's supernatural work through the life of a believer. Several of the gifts mentioned there are for the purpose of revelation—when God discloses something to a believer at the moment of a specific need.

+ A word of knowledge is a supernatural revelation of a fact or detail about a person or situation.

+ A word of wisdom is a supernatural revelation of direction or application in providing wise and sound counsel as to what to do in a situation.

+ Discerning of spirits is the supernatural revelation of what specific spirit is at work in a situation (the human spirit, a demonic spirit, or the Holy Spirit).

When a person is baptized in the Holy Spirit, they become sensitized to these kinds of supernatural disclosures from God. As Ron prayed in tongues, his spirit became even more receptive to what the Holy Spirit was saying to him. As he prayed, he felt a strong urging to leave Huntsville immediately. That was all the information he received.

When God grants revelation about something, He doesn't always explain Himself thoroughly or provide all the details. He gives us everything we need to know to take the next step and make the right decision. Often, He won't let us rest until we have acted upon His guidance. Ron knew he couldn't stay in Huntsville. So he began a series of awkward conversations about leaving early.

He called his wife and said, "Please change my plane ticket. I want to leave right away." He explained to his colleagues that he felt unrest and needed to leave immediately. They were surprised but supported his decision. He checked out of the hotel, traveled to the airport, and stayed the night at a hotel near the airport so he could fly out to Orlando the next day.

During the night, a tornado blew through Huntsville, Alabama. It touched down just outside the hotel where the round-table was being held. It struck the hotel that night, and the point of impact was the very room where Ron had been staying. If Ron had remained, he would most likely have been killed. The other pastors attending the conference were staying several floors below.

When they heard the warnings, they crawled under the staircase in the hallway next to their rooms and successfully weathered the storm without injury.

As Ron flew out the next morning, he was thanking God for the gift of the Holy Spirit in his life and for the protection God provided through the supernatural disclosure (or revelation) of the Holy Spirit.

Ron Johnson is the pastor of One Church in Orlando, Florida. I have heard him teach a rather unique concept about how praying in tongues makes us more sensitive to the information the Holy Spirit wants to give to us. First Corinthians 14:2 teaches us this: *"Anyone who speaks in a tongue does not speak to people but to God. Indeed, no one understands them; they utter mysteries by the Spirit."*

The Holy Spirit prays through us. The Holy Spirit understands what He is praying through our lips, but we don't know the specifics. When we pray in tongues, we often have a burden for a person or a situation, but we don't know exactly what the Spirit of God is praying through us for them; we are uttering *"mysteries by the Spirit."*

Again, in Romans 8:26–27, we read, *"We do not know what we ought to pray for, but the Spirit himself intercedes for us through wordless groans. And he who searches our hearts knows the mind of the Spirit, because the Spirit intercedes for God's people in accordance with the will of God."* The Father searches our hearts and knows the mind of the Spirit. The Holy Spirit knows the Father's will, and He prays through us in accordance with God's will.

Here's what we can deduce from these verses:

+ Praying in the Spirit opens the pipeline of communication between the Holy Spirit within us and God the Father in heaven.

+ The Spirit of God groans out (utters) prayers according to God's will through us. They are mysteries to us, and yet they are precisely what needs to be prayed at the moment to meet the needs of that specific situation.

+ Since the pipeline of communication is open as we pray in this way, we are more ready to receive mysteries and/or revelation of what the Father would like to disclose to us.

Ron Johnson teaches, "God is a reciprocal God. When we allow the Holy Spirit to speak mysteries to the Father through us…—the Father then responds by revealing mysteries to our spirits as well."

Praying in the Spirit sensitizes us to the voice of God. It makes us more aware of His leadings and His promptings. Just as certain conditions and treatments can give the nerves in your skin a heightened sensitivity to touch, so praying in the Spirit provides you with a heightened sensitivity in the spiritual realm. Praying in the Spirit heightens the sensitivity of the "nervous system" in your spirit, so that you can hear things in the Spirit much more clearly than you would otherwise.

I know this probably isn't the best example, but stay with me on this one. Think about dogs. They are known for their sense of smell, but they also have a "very acute sense of hearing." In fact, they hear approximately four times better than humans and can hear much higher and lower frequencies: of 40 to 60,000 Hz compared to a human's ability to hear between 20 and 20,000 Hz.[5] This is why they can hear dog whistles, and we cannot. In the same way, there are spiritual communications outside our hearing, until we train ourselves to hear them.

Somehow, praying in the Spirit increases the frequency range of our spiritual ears. We are more tuned to the interaction between the Holy Spirit within us and the message that heaven is trying to send us.

This may be one of the reasons why the baptism in the Holy Spirit becomes a gateway to the other gifts of the Spirit mentioned in 1 Corinthians 12. Remember, the purpose of the baptism in the Holy Spirit is to clothe you with power. This explosive capacity from God is designed to help you testify to the fact that Jesus has risen from the dead. The miracles God releases through you are confirming signs that prove He is alive and working in the world.

Speaking in tongues occurs at the moment we are baptized in the Holy Spirit. It's a "starter" gift that is the gateway for us to begin to function in the supernatural power of God. How so?

+ *Speaking in tongues is the easiest gift to function in regularly:* When we pray in tongues, we are functioning in the supernatural in our personal and private prayer life. The Holy Spirit is talking to God through us with His words and His concepts.

+ *Speaking in tongues makes us more sensitive in our spirits:* As the channels of communication open up between heaven and earth, our spirits become more tuned in to what God is saying and doing in the world. Being sensitive to the promptings of the Holy Spirit is a major key to functioning in the other gifts.

For instance, one of the gifts of the Spirit (1 Corinthians 12:7–10) is the gift of healing. When I pray for someone to be healed, it helps if I can hear the Holy Spirit tell me who to pray for and what specifically God intends to do for them. Another gift of the Spirit is the gift of prophecy. Prophecy, in its simplest definition, is Holy Spirit-inspired encouragement. We speak words to build up, lift up, and bind up those who need fresh encouragement. Prophecy is directed toward a person and their unique need. How can we prophesy/speak out something that we have not first heard/sensed within our spirits?

If you examine the gifts of the Spirit, each one requires "hearing" from the Holy Spirit before acting in faith based on what we hear.

Speaking in tongues provides a way for me to practice hearing and obeying. When I hear the syllables in my spirit and speak them in prayer, I'm doing the very thing that I do in any of the other supernatural gifts: God speaks, I hear, I obey, and God acts.

The purpose is clear for the baptism in the Holy Spirit. God wants you to live a supernatural life. He wants to give you power to testify of His resurrection. He wants you to eagerly desire to be used in the gifts of the Spirit (1 Corinthians 14:1). Many believers in the Western world have argued that the baptism in the Holy Spirit isn't necessary today. Some have said that the baptism in the Holy Spirit should be sought, but that speaking in tongues isn't necessary. Others believe that all these things (tongues, spiritual gifts, miracles) ceased when the original apostles died. They teach that miracles no longer occur in the life of the believer.

I find all of these arguments fall short of what we actually read in the Scriptures and what I know from experience.

First of all, why would Jesus make this the final thing He said to His disciples, if He didn't intend for the baptism in the Holy Spirit to be important? Remember, this was what Jesus commanded just before He ascended into heaven. How could that command not be perceived as critically important to the mission He had assigned to them?

Second, in the New Testament, every time believers were baptized in the Holy Spirit, supernatural things began to happen. They spoke in tongues. They prophesied. They prayed for the sick and people were healed.

The entirety of the book of Acts is a history of the miraculous work of the Holy Spirit through the life of the believer. Has God suddenly stopped working in this way?

Third, since over half of the world doesn't know Jesus as their Savior, why would God cease providing proof of His resurrection? Don't Muslims need to know that Jesus is the Son of God, risen from the dead? Don't Hindus need more than words to believe? Don't atheists deserve more than moralistic philosophy and/or stories of the power of God that are nearly 2,000 years old?

It suggests to me that perhaps we shouldn't spend so much time figuring out how to operate in the supernatural power of God without having to speak in tongues. Perhaps, instead, we should step boldly into what Jesus commanded His disciples to receive and exercise. Perhaps we should be so hungry to see the power of God released in our generation that we're willing to do whatever we need to do to be used by Him in His power. Perhaps we should so long to see people come to Christ that we're willing to be used as vessels for God to testify to the world of Jesus's resurrection.

A PERSONAL EXPERIENCE

A few years ago, I had a dream. I had just returned from an overseas festival in Africa where we preached the gospel to an unreached people group that had never heard it before. During that week of meetings, I spent a lot of time praying in the Spirit to prepare myself for the ministry that would happen during the festival gatherings. The atmosphere of the meetings was charged with Holy Spirit power; many deaf ears were opened and blind eyes began to see.

My spiritual nervous system was a bit more tuned up than normal, and that sensitivity showed up in one of my dreams. In Acts 2, Simon Peter refers to a prophecy in the book of Joel (written several hundred years earlier) about the outpouring of the Holy Spirit: *"In the last days, God says, I will pour out my Spirit on all people. Your sons and daughters will prophesy, your old men will dream dreams, your young men will see visions"* (Acts 2:17, quoting Joel 2:28).

This is what happened for me. In my dream, I was standing in the fellowship space (we call it our concourse) at Allison Park

Church. There were five or six others standing with me in a circle, and next to me was a tall blonde woman I didn't recognize. As we were standing there and talking, this woman bent over in pain and seemed to be manifesting a demonic spirit. In the Bible, we read about people possessed by demons and how they act out in a way that seems almost beyond their control. This is what was happening in my dream.

When I saw her react this way, I turned to her and spoke. I heard myself saying, "In Jesus's name, come out!" But nothing happened. She continued to manifest this demon as my prayers over her were unsuccessful. In a split second, I was awake. But the dream was still vivid in my mind. In fact, it disturbed me quite a bit. If you have ever found yourself awake after a scary dream, you know this experience of going from a dream state to being really awake. I was trembling and sweating. My adrenaline was pumping, and I knew it would be impossible to go back to sleep.

Instead, I got up and began to pray. I asked God, "Who is this woman? Why did I have this dream about her? More importantly, why did the demon not come out when I used the name of Jesus?" This was actually very disturbing to me. I recalled Ron Johnson's teaching that praying in the Spirit makes us ready to hear from God more clearly, so I began to pray in the Spirit.

I paced back and forth in my living room, praying in my spiritual language. It was 3:30 a.m., but I was wide awake and felt a burden for this woman's situation, whoever she was. As I prayed in tongues, I replayed in my mind the scene from my dream. When I did, the scene shifted. All of a sudden, I saw this same blonde woman, sitting in the corner, crying, rocking back and forth, and holding on to a necklace of some type.

Remember, I was awake at this point, but I was seeing this scene in my mind much like a movie being played for me. To distinguish what was happening, we would say that I was having a "vision" from God. A dream can be a vision from God that we get when we are sleeping. A vision is simply a dream we have when we're awake. Not all dreams are from God. But I knew that this one was.

I stopped praying in the Spirit for a moment, and I asked God, "Why has she not been set free? What is she holding onto as she cries? What needs to happen next?" I stopped praying for a time, as I sang to God in worship. Then I returned to prayer and prayed in my spiritual language as I again tuned in to this vision.

I heard the Holy Spirit say to me, "The necklace she is wearing is the key. She is holding on to this, and what it represents is keeping her bound. If you get her to surrender the necklace, she will be set free."

Then, in the Spirit, I saw that happen. She took off the necklace, stood to her feet, threw her hands in the air, and worshipped God because she was finally free of what had tormented her for so long. I felt a sense of relief and release. I knew that I had heard from God.

This all happened on a Saturday night, and I had a sense that this woman might show up at church the next day. I woke up my wife, Melodie, and explained the dream to her. I'll never forget the look on her face as she rubbed her eyes and tried to figure out why her husband had seemingly gone crazy in the middle of the night.

Then I said to her, "This woman might come to church in the morning. Since I'm speaking tomorrow, you might have to minister to her if she starts to manifest these demons during the message. If she does, here is what you are supposed to do." I explained to her the significance of the necklace. I told her, "The necklace is the key; you have to get her to give up the necklace." Needless to say, Melodie was a bit unnerved but was willing to deal with the situation if it arose.

Sunday morning, just before the start of the service, I was standing in the café in our concourse. As I turned, I saw a tall blonde woman enter the building. It was the woman I had seen in my dream. I turned to my wife and said, "That's her! That's the woman I saw in my dream." So my wife went over and began to visit with the woman. Melodie welcomed her to church, and they got to know one another.

I went into the service and began to lead and prepare to speak. While my wife continued to talk with the woman, the woman bent over as if she was in pain (just like I had seen in the dream). She told my wife, "I think I'm going to be sick." Melodie led her to a private space where the blonde woman could catch her breath and they could talk and pray. Melodie prayed for her and every time she said the name of Jesus, the woman seemed to get worse. She groaned and bent over as Melodie mentioned Jesus's name. It was obvious that a demonic spirit was affecting the woman's life.

After a time of prayer and conversation, Melodie remembered my instructions: "You have to get her to remove that necklace because something about that necklace is keeping her bound."

My wife inquired about the necklace: "I notice that when you bend over, you hold onto your necklace. Does that necklace mean something to you?"

The woman replied, "Yes, my boyfriend gave it to me. He abused me sexually, physically, and emotionally, and just recently left me. I feel so used and alone. So I sit in the corner in my apartment and I cry and hold onto this necklace as a way of remembering him and what he did to me."

Melodie responded, "Would you be willing to give me that necklace? And as you give it to me, you need to choose to let your boyfriend go. Turn your heart over to God. Let God heal the pain inside. He wants to set you free, but you have to choose to surrender to Him and let Jesus restore your soul."

"Yes," the woman responded, "I'll give you the necklace. I probably should give you the bracelets as well, because he gave these to me also." She took them off one at a time and placed them in Melodie's hands. Then she prayed the salvation prayer and gave her life to Jesus Christ. As soon as she finished the prayer, she stood up and lifted her hands to God. Tears were streaming down her face as the inner healing process began.

Jesus set her free just like I saw in the dream!

This is why the baptism in the Holy Spirit is so important. Through the infilling of the Holy Spirit, God gives us access to information and revelation that we would never have in any other way. He loved that woman so much that He went to the trouble to wake me up with a dream about her plight. As I prayed in the Spirit, He unfolded to me the words of knowledge I needed to provide the pathway out of her torment. As the service continued that morning, the Holy Spirit ministered to this woman as He worked through Melodie to lead her to a place of freedom.

In the same way, God wants to use you to impact people by the power of God. He wants to speak to you and through you. He wants to work miracles through your prayers. He wants to release healing and freedom through you. Because the Holy Spirit lives within you, you have the potential to do anything that God asks you to do. The Holy Spirit wants to perform miracles through you.

All of this is possible when we are clothed with power; when we receive the fire clothes of Jesus through the baptism in the Holy Spirit.

CHAPTER SIX DISCUSSION QUESTIONS

1. Have you ever seen a dog respond to a dog whistle? Is it hard for you to believe the dog can hear something that you can't?

2. Is it possible for you to become a little more sensitive to some sounds rather than others? (Example: Mothers are sensitive to the cries of their newborns.) Can you think of other examples?

3. What makes us most sensitive to the voice of the Holy Spirit? How do you know that you are hearing His voice?

4. What's the weirdest dream you have ever had? Read Acts 2:17–18. Have you ever had God speak to you in a dream or a vision?

5. How can we be more aware and open to what God wants to communicate with us this week?

SEVEN
IT'S RELEVANT

The cause of weakness in your Christian life is that you want to work it out partly, and let God help you. And that cannot be. You must become utterly helpless, to let God work, and God will work gloriously.
—Andrew Murray[6]

Back in the 1990s, it was our practice at Allison Park Church to hold a Sunday night service. Sunday nights were different from our normal Sunday morning services. We gave a teaching, but the atmosphere was designed for people to have an experience with God with extra time for them to worship and pray.

One Sunday night, Leah Ferguson was teaching. As she gave the message, she paused and shared a "word of knowledge." Now, remember that the baptism in the Holy Spirit is the gateway to living a supernatural life. As a person learns to partner with the Holy Spirit, they start to function in the various gifts of the Holy Spirit that are described in 1 Corinthians 12:7–10. One of those gifts is the word of knowledge, which is the revelation to a person of a fact about someone or something that could not be known naturally.

Leah said, "Someone is here tonight who has experienced deep pain. God is getting ready to heal you in that area. As you humble yourself before Him, He is going to touch that area of pain and scarring and begin complete healing in that area of your life." After she said this, she went on with her teaching, and none of us thought anything about it. In the audience that night was a man by the name of Kevin Kuchta.

Kevin had been attending Allison Park Church for only a few months. He had a physical condition that caused him to experience pain in his bones. The bone disease, avascular necrosis, was caused by medicine he had received for an intestinal disease. The medication actually caused major portions of his femurs to die, leaving the surviving bone to become stressed, brittle, and susceptible to fracture. He had undergone multiple surgeries to address the disease in his legs, and yet the problem had not been corrected. Modern medicine can do many incredible things, but it can't bring tissue back from the dead. He had deep pain and physical scarring because of the condition and required many orthopedic surgeries.

The most obvious way you could see the physical impact on Kevin was that he couldn't get around without either a wheelchair or crutches. When Kevin heard the word of knowledge from Leah, something inside of him began to burn. The Holy Spirit spoke to him and said, "That word was for you!"

At the end of the service, Kevin responded to Leah's altar call. He used his crutches to get himself to the front of the auditorium. He did what was requested in the word of knowledge. He humbled himself. He recounts that he doesn't remember how he got down on the floor. Usually, that would take help from someone—someone strong.

There Kevin lay facedown before the Lord. "Then it happened," he recalls. "I felt the power of God come all over me. It was so strong that I began to tremble violently. My entire body would shake for a season, and then it would subside. Then again it would come on me like a wave. I would shake, and then it would subside. This happened about ten to twelve times. I was scared, but I kept hearing, 'Be still and know that I am God.' On the final time, I felt a searing pain in my back right where my kidneys are located. When the pain stopped, I felt a sense of peace."

Kevin felt God speaking to him again saying, "Stand up!"

Kevin argued, "But, God, I'm not sure how I can get up off the floor without help. It's impossible for me to do this." Again, Kevin sensed that inner voice of the Holy Spirit telling him to stand, so he obeyed. He pushed himself to his knees, then tried to get from his knees to his feet. To his surprise, his legs held his weight without pain and with free range of motion. He stood straight up. At the time, I was standing at the front of the auditorium, talking to another person. Almost everyone had departed because it was about thirty minutes after the service had ended. Kevin was new to the church. When I saw him standing there, I said, "Hi, Kevin," but it didn't dawn on me that he was standing without crutches since I didn't know him that well.

He said to me, "Hey, Pastor Jeff! Look at me! I am standing right here!"

"Yes," I said, "I can see that," not really sure what in the world he meant.

Then Kevin pointed to his crutches lying on the floor. "I'm standing here!" Kevin explained as he saw my obvious confusion.

I asked, "What happened? Did you experience a healing miracle?"

"I think so!" Kevin responded with shock and awe.

He said that he was scared. I didn't understand why until he said, "What if this isn't real? If this is just adrenaline or something, and I tried to walk, I could break my leg. My left femur has fractured in the past just by moving myself on my living-room couch."

He was confused about what he had experienced and scared that he was wrong about his healing. I asked him what exactly had happened. As he described it to me, he realized that he had just experienced what was, indeed, a miracle! Then it really dawned on us both. What a moment, and what a mixture of emotions. Joy! Tears! Laughter! Shock! Gratitude! It was quite a way to end a Sunday night service!

Kevin picked up his crutches and carried them out the back door. I will never, ever, forget that moment. It was a genuine, verifiable, supernatural event that had happened right in our church! And it happened as a result of the Holy Spirit working in the life of one person to prompt a miracle in the life of another.

By the way, Kevin is a scientist. He normally rolled into work in his wheelchair. You can imagine the impact when he walked into work on Monday morning: no wheelchair, no crutches, healed. The scientists had no explanation for what had happened to Kevin, but they could see visible proof that Jesus is alive and is still doing miracles in the world today. I asked Kevin to follow up with his doctors. Later, he told me that his surgeons examined him and were amazed. The chief surgeon, after examining his range of motion and comparative X-rays, looked at him and said, "Sometimes you just have to call a miracle, a 'miracle'!"

I have just described for you one of the most amazing instances I have ever seen of the Holy Spirit's work through the life of a surrendered believer. If every story we heard about the Holy Spirit ended this way, there would never be anything controversial whatsoever about this experience. But not everyone has had an experience like Kevin's. Some have been in a room where someone expressed a spiritual gift and it was either weird, awkward, or confusing, or it created a sense of pressure or manipulation in the way it was expressed.

This was the problem in the Corinthian church. The apostle Paul, when writing 1 Corinthians, was addressing some of the internal struggles the church in Corinth was experiencing. One of the problems was the misuse and abuse of the supernatural gifts and experiences of the Holy Spirit.

What was going on? Their services were a spiritual circus. If you had entered the weekly services at the church in Corinth, you would have seen nothing but confusion. Some people were interrupting the service by standing up and randomly speaking in tongues. Others were trying to take over the service by speaking out words of prophecy for lengthy periods of time. One person would be speaking publicly, and then another person would try to talk over them, and there would be a "war for airtime," so to speak.

People were leaving services frustrated, confused, and wondering what it was all about. What was most concerning about this environment was the impact it was having on the Corinthian church's ability to reach people who needed Christ. Paul expressed it like this: *"If the whole church comes together and everyone speaks in tongues, and inquirers or unbelievers come in, will they not say that you are out of your mind?"* (1 Corinthians 14:23).

This may be the unspoken danger you feel as you read this book. You might be thinking, "I'm with you. I believe the power of God is needed as a witness to the resurrection. I believe the Holy Spirit is needed in the life of every believer. I believe that speaking in tongues is an experience for today. But I'm afraid that if I start to live this out or lead people in these teachings, our church is going to become a crazy charismatic environment that is awkward, confusing, and limited in its ability to reach out to those who are lost."

How do I make this work in my life and not become part of a spiritual crazy house? The instructions that we find in 1 Corinthians 14 provide the pathway to proper function and use. Now, the content of this chapter is less about the baptism in the Holy Spirit and more about the down-the-line impact of the baptism in the Holy Spirit. Once you are baptized in the Holy Spirit, you will begin to function in the gifts of the Holy Spirit, as well.

Once people begin to flow in the gifts of the Holy Spirit, they also need to learn some principles for how to function appropriately in those gifts. This is what Paul carefully outlined in 1 Corinthians 14. You may want to put this book down for a moment, find that chapter in the Bible, and read it. Then, come back and read through the various principles in the following pages.

PRINCIPLE 1: EXPECTATION

Follow the way of love and eagerly desire the gifts of the Spirit.   (1 Corinthians 14:1)

In the first verse of this chapter, Paul mentions two things that must be kept in balance. Some want to (1) follow the way of love. They want to make sure that everything is done with others in mind. They want to design church services that people can relate to and understand.

They want their spiritual experiences to draw people to Jesus, not turn them away. They want to make the Bible and the gospel relevant to those who are far from God.

Others want to (2) eagerly desire the gifts of the Spirit. They want to see every aspect of God's power released in their lives. If there's a spiritual experience to be had, they want to experience it. They want every drop of the Holy Spirit to be manifested in their lives. They want to design church services where people have the liberty and freedom to soak in the presence of God and experience the transformative power of the Holy Spirit.

Too many times, we're on one side or the other of this equation. Paul teaches that we need to have both to function biblically. It isn't enough to love people; we also need to *"eagerly desire gifts of the Spirit.*" It also isn't enough to want to flow in the powerful gifts of the Spirit and not be aware of the need to love and reach out to people. Both must be kept in balance. Both must be present in our passionate pursuit.

Which one do you currently lean toward? How can you make sure you are intentionally pursuing both? Are you focused on loving people? Are you eagerly and intentionally expecting to be used in the supernatural?

PRINCIPLE 2: EDIFICATION

For anyone who speaks in a tongue does not speak to people but to God. Indeed, no one understands them; they utter mysteries by the Spirit. But the one who prophesies speaks to people for their strengthening, encouraging and comfort.

(1 Corinthians 14:2–3)

Whenever God works supernaturally through the life of one person to meet the needs of another, it is always for the purpose of edification. What does it mean to edify? The verses define it: to strengthen, encourage, and comfort. Some have said it like this: to build up, to cheer up, and to lift up. This is the standard and motivation for being used in the power of God.

My hunger to be used by God and to experience the power of the Holy Spirit is not just for me. Yes, God wants to heal me, to restore me, to empower me, to use me. Yes, God wants to use my lips to pray supernatural prayers. It's amazing to experience the presence of God Himself in our lives.

But when we are with others, we have to aim our experiences with the Holy Spirit toward the edification of everyone present in the room. When I pray in private, I can feel free to speak in tongues, sing, or shout for joy to go deeper into God's presence. But when I'm with others (especially those who are not yet believers), I need to consider how my actions and responses to the Holy Spirit are affecting them.

PRINCIPLE 3: NORMALIZATION

Again, if the trumpet does not sound a clear call, who will get ready for battle? So it is with you. Unless you speak intelligible words with your tongue, how will anyone know what you are saying? You will just be speaking into the air. Undoubtedly there are all sorts of languages in the world, yet none of them is without meaning. If then I do not grasp the meaning of what someone is saying, I am a foreigner to the speaker, and the speaker is a foreigner to me. So it is with you. Since you are eager for gifts of the Spirit, try to excel in those that build up the church.   (1 Corinthians 14:8–12)

This may be the biggest issue of all when it comes to functioning appropriately with spiritual gifts. Whatever we say or do has to be expressed in such a way that it can be understood and received by those who hear us. Remember, the goal is to build up those who are present. We need to fashion what we say and do so others can understand it and apply it.

I grew up in a Pentecostal church and experienced many services that were a lot like the "spiritual circus" in the church at Corinth. What was typical in a lot of these events was this: Whoever was being used in a spiritual gift would suddenly become a different person. Their voice would tremble, and the volume would rise. It was startling, emotional, and sometimes a bit scary.

What I believed about the supernatural was this: When God used someone, it was like a lightning bolt hit them. They would lose control of who they were. God would take over and make them do and say things that were beyond understanding. It was like detonating a powerful spiritual explosive that would spray all kinds of spiritual debris everywhere.

Often, I didn't understand how what was happening could benefit anyone in the room, but I didn't want to argue with what the Holy Spirit was doing, so I endured it and ignored it. I wasn't against it, but, honestly, I wasn't really interested in having an experience that seemed so odd and out of place. The way in which spiritual gifts were used, in my experience, did several things to me:

+ I believed that functioning in the supernatural was only for a special class of people who were eerily in touch with God in a way that I was not.

+ I was inoculated against wanting to be used in spiritual gifts because I was unwilling to become so emotional and demonstrative in front of others.

+ I began to believe that spiritual gifts could only happen in Pentecostal worship services. I never heard stories of their functioning outside of a church building.

+ I was hesitant to bring my friends to church with me because I didn't know how to explain to them the weird emotional explosions that might happen during the service.

I have since learned that functioning in spiritual gifts doesn't have to be spooky, emotional, or spoken in old King James English. In fact, what I see written in 1 Corinthians 14 is that the explosive way these gifts are so often practiced is potentially a hindrance to their proper use.

What I teach people now is that spiritual gifts should be used in a normal tone of voice, and out of your authentic personality. When God starts to move through you, you may feel emotions well up within you, but you are capable of managing your emotions in order to convey a message or word of encouragement in the most effective way for the people who are listening.

Spiritual gifts aren't released when a lightning bolt strikes you; spiritual gifts are released when you decide to partner with the inner prompting of the Holy Spirit to speak out and believe for

God to work in the life of another person. We should expect that God will release the gifts of the Holy Spirit through us during a worship service. But even more than that, we should expect that God will release the gifts of the Holy Spirit in our everyday lives, Monday through Friday, and Saturday, as well.

We should practice using the gifts in a normal way. What I like to teach is this: If you were in a grocery store, and God spoke to you about someone you saw in one of the aisles, how would you use that gift? Hopefully, you wouldn't close your eyes, shake, lift your voice, and start to say, "Thus says the Lord...."

Wouldn't that totally freak people out?

Rather, you might approach that person in a humble tone. Introduce yourself. Explain what happened to you as you walked down the aisle. Explain how the Holy Spirit prompted you to say something. Present your message in a sensitive way, aware of your surroundings and in touch with the person's reactions and response.

This is the way the Holy Spirit wants to work.

PRINCIPLE 4: EXPLANATION

Now, brothers and sisters, if I come to you and speak in tongues, what good will I be to you, unless I bring you some revelation or knowledge or prophecy or word of instruction? Even in the case of lifeless things that make sounds, such as the pipe or harp, how will anyone know what tune is being played unless there is a distinction in the notes?

(1 Corinthians 14:6–7)

I have found that most people are open to the supernatural, especially if the atmosphere they are in feels safe. People don't feel safe when they don't understand what is happening around them, especially if, all of a sudden, someone gets really emotional and does something unusual or unique in close proximity to them.

Now, I realize that safety isn't our only goal. We want power. We want transformation. We want to see people healed, restored, and visited by the presence of God. But I believe we can do all of that, and at the same time make people feel safe enough that they can relax and remain open to what God is doing.

The key to feeling safe is having someone there to interpret what is going on. If we slow the process down enough to say, "This is what is happening; this is what the Bible teaches; and this is why this is important," then we gain the trust of those we are trying to reach.

PRINCIPLE 5: INCLUSION

The spirits of prophets are subject to the control of prophets. For God is not a God of disorder but of peace—as in all the congregations of the Lord's people.
(1 Corinthians 14:32–33)

When I teach this, I get some pushback from people who come from traditional Pentecostal backgrounds. They say, "When the Holy Spirit comes on me, I can't control how the message comes out. In fact, if I try to control it, I limit what the Holy Spirit wants to do."

My response is always to go back to the Bible. Paul teaches in this 1 Corinthians passage that those who are prophets (meaning they are speaking under the inspiration of the Holy Spirit) *can* control the function of their own spirits. As they hear from God, they can manage the way that message is delivered. *"For God is not a God of disorder but of peace."*

I have titled this principle "Inclusion" for a reason. For over a hundred years, Pentecostal churches have practiced the use of spiritual gifts in worship services by an interruption in the service.

From the days of the Azusa Street Mission—when people gathered for worship on the top floor of an old hall with sawdust floors, wooden benches, and no electronic sound system—the practice has been for a person to stand up in the service, take the floor, and declare a word from God. Sometimes, one person interrupts the service by speaking in tongues. Then another person interrupts the service by interpreting those tongues. This has been the normal function in Pentecostal churches for years.

After pastoring at Allison Park Church for over a decade, I realized that this interruptive style, perhaps more than anything else, was what made people feel unsafe. They never knew who would speak, from where in the auditorium, what they would say, or even whether or not the speaker was credible and trustworthy. Many times, people couldn't hear the speaker or couldn't understand the message because the speaker wasn't speaking into a microphone. It was messy and confusing.

That's when I realized: The world has changed since 1906.

No one ever stands in the middle of a crowded room and shouts out a message. That may have been the culture of the day before sound systems, stages, and so forth. Town-hall meetings and small country venues were the order of the day, but not anymore. That's why an interruption in the service with someone shouting out a message from God seems so unusual and unsettling in our current culture.

In response, at our church, we changed how we function with spiritual gifts in our worship services. When someone feels they have a word or prophecy, instead of shouting from their seat, they simply come to one of our pastoral team members and share with them what they are sensing. Then, we either have them come up onto the platform to share, or we convey the message to the congregation on their behalf.

This one change has done more to make everyone feel safe than anything else when it comes to our function. And this one change has led to several other things:

+ Quiet and shy people who would never have shouted from their seats are being used in spiritual gifts.

+ People who attend our church feel safe and are bringing their friends to church in greater numbers.

+ We are teaching how to use the gifts in a normal tone and an explained fashion.

+ More and more people are using spiritual gifts in their everyday lives.

PRINCIPLE 6: DEMONSTRATION

And you should imitate me, just as I imitate Christ.
(1 Corinthians 11:1 NLT)

Most of this chapter is spent on bringing balance to areas of practice where there is excess. But I want to emphasize that there can be no *balance* without a *beginning*. There's no need for parameters when nothing is practiced. Perhaps you have heard it stated, "Better to have wildfire than no fire at all."

When it comes to actual fire, I'm not sure that is true! But when it comes to the working of the Holy Spirit, I believe it is absolutely valid. It's possible to take so many precautions to avoid offending or scaring people that we totally eliminate any opportunity for God to operate in our midst. It's actually impossible to model for people something that we don't practice or pursue ourselves.

One of the things I so appreciated about my parents was that they had a faith that was more than just words. I'll never forget the day my dad came home from visiting someone at the hospital. One of the members of our church had become ill and wasn't expected to live through the night. My father was called to the bedside to comfort the family as they watched their father die. Standing beside the hospital bed, my dad reminded the family, "Doctors provide a prognosis, but God has the final word. We can still believe God for a miracle."

As they prayed, the Holy Spirit moved, and Mr. Thurston not only survived the night, he walked out of the hospital the next day—totally healed. This moment impressed me as a teenager more than I can express. Amazing thoughts swirled through my head: "God must truly be real! My dad knows God and knows how to pray! Following Jesus isn't boring; it's an adventure!"

I'm the father of five kids (and now the grandfather of my first grandchild). My desire is to demonstrate to them a faith that has more than just principles and values. I want to give them a faith that carries transformational power. As a pastor, I want to introduce my people to more than just good teaching, descriptions of stories from long ago, and encouraging thoughts for their lives. My desire is to introduce them to the *person* of the Holy Spirit and to demonstrate before them a life that is lived out of Holy Spirit power.

PRINCIPLE 7: PREPARATION

What then shall we say, brothers and sisters? When you come together, each of you has a hymn, or a word of instruction, a revelation, a tongue or an interpretation. Everything must be done so that the church may be built up.

(1 Corinthians 14:26)

Because the Holy Spirit lives within every believer, and since He is never without the capacity to demonstrate His power, we should anticipate that He will constantly show up in our lives. It's an everyday expectation; a moment-by-moment anticipation.

Every time we attend a church service or a small group, or encounter someone in need, we are living moments filled with divine potential because the Holy Spirit fills our lives.

Bruce Wilkinson has written one of the best books I have ever read about this kind of preparation to live a supernatural life. The book is titled *You Were Born for This: 7 Keys to a Life of Predictable Miracles*. He paints this picture for us:

> You were born to be a living link between Heaven and earth. You were born to be God's ambassador in the Everyday Miracle Territory, making Him visible in unforgettable ways. The miraculous touches of Heaven that God wants to accomplish His will come in all sizes, but mostly they'll be of the personal, everyday sort that you can be a part of. Why? Because God passionately desires to show Himself strong for you and through you, and because every person you meet has a significant need that only God can meet.[7]

You are a member of God's "miracle delivery system"—a phrase Bruce coined in this book. I love that picture of what we are. You are a carrier of the Holy Spirit. He is ready to move in your life and in the lives of those around you at any given moment. Therefore, we should live tuned up, prayed up, and ready to be used by God!

CHAPTER SEVEN DISCUSSION QUESTIONS

1. What is the worst customer service experience you have ever had? What made it so bad?

2. In your opinion, are most churches aware of what outsiders feel? Are we, as the church, good at creating environments where people feel welcome and safe?

3. How do you make people feel comfortable when they enter your home?

4. What kinds of things do you feel are necessary to reach an unbeliever when God calls you to minister to someone who is brand-new to God or to church?

5. What will happen to the church if it ever stops creating room for the Holy Spirit to move in our environments? What's the balance?

6. Have you ever seen this done really well—where someone ministered to you in a powerful, Holy Spirit way, and yet maintained humility and sensitivity? Describe this moment and why it so impacted you.

EIGHT
IT'S TRANSFORMATIONAL

Sometimes it seems safer to have just enough God to get to heaven, but not so much that he radically alters our lives.
—Chris Hodges[8]

One of the most heartbreaking things I have done as a pastor is to walk with someone through a painful divorce or the breakdown of what had been a seemingly vibrant relationship.

One instance, in particular, stands out to me as perhaps the most shocking and agonizing heartbreak I have ever seen.

I was in the room when my friend received the news. Not only was his wife cheating on him; she was cheating on him with his best friend! After the initial shock, questions flooded his mind. "How long has this been going on? When did it start? How did it start? Why? How could you? What do I do now? How do I even begin to function again?"

No physical earthquake could have rocked his world more. It was a life-altering moment, without question. The only choice he had was whether to let this painful disappointment alter his life in a way that would destroy him or let it lead him to a place that would make him a better man.

Now, I know that seems like an extreme oversimplification. Even as I wrote that last sentence, I realized how insensitive it sounds. After all, he did nothing to deserve what happened to him. He wasn't a bad guy or a poor husband. The destructiveness of that moment had little to do with his choices. It had to do with the choices of those around him—those closest to him, mind you! So how could his decision have anything to do with the destructive potential of that situation?

Please understand that I'm not saying his choices could have prevented the damage done by others. The pain of that moment was 100 percent a result of the actions of others. But the trajectory of his life from that moment forward was very much dependent on the choices he made about how he would respond to it.

Charles Swindoll is famous for saying, "Life is 10 percent what happens to you and 90 percent how you respond to it." I watched as my friend responded like a champion. Actually, he made three decisions that truly saved and changed his life:

1. He immersed himself in the Bible. Every time he faced a painful memory or envisioned the image of his best friend and his wife together, he redirected his thoughts toward memorizing the Word of God. He told me, "That's the only thing that kept me from going crazy."

2. He became an active participant in a men's small group. These guys became his armor bearers and stood with him in the lowest moments of his life.

3. He filled his life with worship. His job involved driving a truck, so he had a lot of free moments to think during the day. When he wasn't memorizing Scripture, he spent hours in worship: music blaring away in the cab of the truck with him singing at the top of his lungs. And since he was baptized in the Holy Spirit, he would also pray in the Spirit throughout the day.

What I can tell you is this: Not only did he make it through the worst trial of his entire life, he came through on the other side of it whole and powerful. Prior to this tragedy, he was a tepid or lukewarm believer, at best. He attended church. He served on occasion. But his walk with God was shallow.

Something happened to him when the pain of the moment drove him into a place of desperation. As he practiced the daily disciplines of partnership with God, he became incredibly mature and strong. Honestly, his walk with God challenged me. Every time I was around him, I was affected by his spirit.

And somehow, after all of this, God gave him the grace to forgive his wife. She repented. She worked like crazy to earn back his trust. She joined him in his desperate pursuit of the presence and promises of God, and over time, the wound healed and their marriage was restored. Two decades later, I can tell you they are still married and actively serving God together. Their three kids have been raised in a home that could have been broken for good but has now stood the test of time.

Several chapters ago, I mentioned the Greek word that Jesus used to describe the Holy Spirit, *paraclete*. In this Scription, it is translated as "another advocate." *"And I will ask the Father, and he will give you another advocate to help you and be with you forever—the Spirit of truth"* (John 14:16–17). A paraclete is someone who lives within us and imparts resources to us that we don't have on our own. A parasite lives within us to rob us of our strength, but a paraclete lives within us to impart to us his strength.

Jesus used another example to describe this close relationship: *"I am the vine; you are the branches. If you remain in me and I in you, you will bear much fruit; apart from me you can do nothing"* (John 15:5). The imagery is clear. Life flows through the vine, like sap through the trunk of a tree. As long as the branch is connected to the vine, it is connected to the source and flow of life. When it is disconnected, it dies.

A connected branch has capacity. It remains strong. It flourishes. It produces leaves and fruit in abundance. A connected branch has life that isn't self-produced; it comes from another source, the vine. A disconnected branch is not only dead, it is unproductive. *"Apart from me,"* Jesus declared, *"you can do nothing."*

Connected to the vine, I can do anything. Disconnected from the vine, I can do nothing!

Here's the application. When I choose to surrender my life to Jesus Christ, and I put my faith in who He is, I become connected to "the vine." It's like being grafted into the trunk of the vine because previously we were *"dead in* [our] *transgressions and sins"* (Ephesians 2:1), but now God has made us alive in Christ (see Ephesians 2:5–6).

As soon as our dead branch connects to the vine, the Holy Spirit ignites something inside of us. Not only are we saved from the consequences of our sin and forgiven and made righteous in the sight of God, we are also regenerated or infused with life on the inside. Jesus said in John 3 that we are *"born again"* (verse 3), or "born of the Spirit."

A new reality has come into effect in our lives. We now have a reservoir of life to draw from within our own being, and since the Holy Spirit is such a dynamic person, He adds to us everything we need for any situation we face. Whenever we have a lack, we can look to the Holy Spirit because He is and He has all that we need.

HE SHARES WITH US HIS DISPOSITION

If we stick with this metaphor of the vine and branches, we see another example of the outcome of this relationship. The apostle Paul tells us the kind of fruit we can expect in our lives as a result of this connection: *"The fruit of the Spirit is love, joy, peace, forbearance, kindness, goodness, faithfulness, gentleness and self-control"* (Galatians 5:22–23).

Here's the fantastic news: The Holy Spirit provides everything we need for every situation!

+ When I'm weary, tired, discouraged, and ready to give up, I have no joy on the inside. However, the Holy Spirit never lacks joy; it's always His disposition. Since He lives inside of me, He's willing to share His joy with me. All I have to do is tap into His presence.

+ If you're a parent, trying to balance work and home and activities, and you have run out of patience with all the challenges you face, the Holy Spirit is perfectly patient. When you choose to worship or pray in the Spirit, He will release more than enough patience into your soul.

+ When you're anxious and tied up in knots over a situation, the Holy Spirit never has anxiety. He only knows peace. He has more than enough peace to share.

Do not be anxious about anything, but in every situation, by prayer and petition, with thanksgiving, present your requests to God. And the peace of God, which transcends all understanding, will guard your hearts and your minds in Christ Jesus.   (Philippians 4:6–7)

The peace of God that is given to us is not independent of the Holy Spirit's work in our lives. It is a quality of soul that is deposited within us because of His work in our lives. So when you take time every day to pray, you aren't only practicing an excellent spiritual discipline but you're also activating the Holy Spirit's work in your life and intentionally accessing His disposition (the fruits of the Spirit).

HE SHARES WITH US HIS CAPACITY

Here's a second piece of fantastic news: Not only does the Holy Spirit have an amazing and unshakable disposition, He also has precise and powerful solutions for every problem we could ever face. We typically call these solutions the "gifts of the Spirit." Notice this description:

> *Now to each one the manifestation of the Spirit is given for the common good. To one there is given through the Spirit a message of wisdom, to another a message of knowledge by means of the same Spirit, to another faith by the same Spirit, to another gifts of healing by that one Spirit, to another miraculous powers, to another prophecy, to another distinguishing between spirits, to another speaking in different kinds of tongues, and to still another the interpretation of tongues. All these are the work of one and the same Spirit, and he distributes them to each one, just as he determines.*
>
> (1 Corinthians 12:7–11)

Notice a few things that are taught here:

+ The Spirit gives these gifts for the common good (everyone's benefit).

+ Since the Spirit gives these gifts, we know that the Spirit possesses these gifts.

+ All of these supernatural solutions are the work of the same Spirit.

+ The Spirit gives these gifts to each of us as we need or as He determines.

In conclusion, the Holy Spirit has all the power we need, all the timely information we need, and all the solutions we need for any and all situations we face. He is willing to share that power, that information, and those solutions with us at the moment we need them. I'm not sure who taught me this definition for the gifts of the Spirit, but I like it: "The gifts of the Spirit are divine explosions of God's power through the life of a surrendered believer to meet human need at precisely the time it is needed." Because we have the Holy Spirit—or because He has us—we can expect Him to explode on the scene with His provision at just the right time.

Every day we walk around with the third person of the Trinity alive within our souls. The same Spirit who raised Jesus from the dead gives life to our mortal bodies. (See Romans 8:11.) This means that the potential for an outbreak of God's power resides in you every day, every moment, in every place, no matter the situation.

Can you imagine what a tragedy it is that so many Holy Spirit-empowered believers simply choose to live out of their own strength and solutions rather than out of His? What a shame that we don't realize and access the capacity He wants to make available to us! Too many of us live as if the Holy Spirit is a last resort for help when a crisis becomes more than we can handle, or as if there were no Holy Spirit at all!

Every day we have the potential to access God's precise and powerful solutions to our problems if we tune in to the Holy Spirit's operation within our lives. This is critical, not only for us to live overcoming and godly lives but also for the world around us to receive ministry from God through us. You and I possess the potential to change the world, to see miracles released, and to have signs and wonders manifest to prove that Jesus is alive.

What that requires is a daily approach to activating the Holy Spirit's work as we worship, pray, and live.

HE SHARES WITH US HIS UNDERSTANDING

The final piece of fantastic news I want to mention here is that the Holy Spirit always has complete understanding and incredible insight into whatever we need to know. Jesus encouraged His disciples with this on the final night before His crucifixion. He had let them know He was going to leave them and how much better it would be for them after He sent them the Holy Spirit.

> *All this I have spoken while still with you. But the Advocate, the Holy Spirit, whom the Father will send in my name, will teach you all things and will remind you of everything I have said to you. Peace I leave with you; my peace I give you. I do not give to you as the world gives. Do not let your hearts be troubled and do not be afraid.* (John 14:25–27)

The Holy Spirit will teach you *all* things and will remind you of *everything*. When I'm confused and don't know what to do, the Holy Spirit knows. When I face a situation that is more complicated than I can figure out, it isn't complicated to Him. When I need to understand who God is or what the Bible is teaching in a difficult passage, the Holy Spirit is there to give the insight I need. When I'm in an argument with my wife and I can't seem to figure out what to do or say, the Holy Spirit has perfect understanding of who Melodie is, what she needs, and how I need to respond to her.

The Holy Spirit knows everything! And He's willing to share what He knows with me.

A few years ago, I decided to preach a series of sermons about the Holy Spirit. It was a Friday night, and I had prepared my message for the weekend. My goal was to communicate the concept I just outlined: that the Holy Spirit has perfect understanding and wants to share it with us in our moments of need.

As I was falling asleep, I was praying about my message and meditating on the truth of the statements Jesus made in John 14. In the middle of the night, I woke up with an overwhelming sense of the presence of God. Actually, I woke myself up praying in tongues. Now, I know that last statement makes me sound incredibly spiritual, so let me clarify that this has only happened two or three times in my entire life. Most of the time, when I wake up in the middle of the night, I'm thinking about pizza or dreaming some crazy dream about a movie I watched the night before.

But on this occasion, I woke up hearing myself speaking in tongues. As I awoke, I felt the inner whisper of the Holy Spirit say something very specific to me: "When you speak to your people this weekend, tell them I am so much smarter than they are."

When I felt this prompting, I laughed out loud. Then I heard Him speak to me again: "Tell them I'm so much smarter than they are, and I want them to know that." I thought about the logic of this statement. At first, it sounded almost arrogant. But it wasn't arrogance; it was just a statement of fact. He *is* so much smarter than we are!

"For my thoughts are not your thoughts, neither are your ways my ways," declares the LORD. *"As the heavens are higher than the earth, so are my ways higher than your ways and my thoughts than your thoughts."*   (Isaiah 55:8–9)

The next day, when I spoke to my church, I told them what the Holy Spirit had directed me to say. "The Holy Spirit wants you to know that He is so much smarter than you are, and He wants to share with you what He knows. Too often you're depending on your own thoughts to solve unsolvable problems. But the Holy Spirit isn't just a little smarter than you. He is much smarter than you. It's actually not even close. You aren't even in the same ballpark when it comes to what He knows. So stop depending on your own thoughts, and ask for His help."

When I declared this, there was a breakthrough in the atmosphere. We all laughed out loud together at this obvious truth, and then we began to worship. We asked the Holy Spirit to help us with our problems. The pressure lifted. The stress disappeared. Life and peace began to flow, because He is so much smarter than we are, and when we trust Him, we can access all we need for the moment we are in.

IT'S ABOUT LIVING OUT OF A DIFFERENT SOURCE

This understanding about who the Holy Spirit is, and how He works in my life to lead me, empower me, and transform me, has changed my approach to life. I no longer approach my daily devotional time just from a place of spiritual discipline. Yes, I realize that spiritual disciplines like prayer, Bible reading, and fasting are critical to spiritual formation. Growth happens as I learn to discipline myself in my relationship with God. This duty to pursue God is important, but it's so much more than just a duty, and so much more than just discipline.

If I approach my daily time with God as an encounter with a *Person*, then my expectations are much different. My devotional life isn't something I do for God, a set of prayers I pray, or lists of Bible verses I read. My devotional life is activating the operation of the Holy Spirit in my life.

- ✦ I don't just read the Bible; I read the Bible with Him for His insight and illumination.

- ✦ I don't just pray; I pray with Him. Actually, as I pray in the Spirit, I let Him pray through me with precision according to the will of God.

- ✦ When I finish that time of devotion, I know I enter my day ready to live out of His disposition, prepared to deliver His solutions to a needy world, and aware that He is so much smarter than I am in every situation I face.

CHAPTER EIGHT DISCUSSION QUESTIONS

1. Describe a moment in your life when your cell phone ran out of power at just the wrong time.

2. Read John 15:1–7. What are your observations from these verses about the power source for your spiritual life? List at least three things from these verses.

3. Read Galatians 5:22–23. How does it make you feel to know that the Holy Spirit always has these qualities in His possession?

4. What practical steps are involved in accessing the disposition and capacity of the Holy Spirit in these areas of life?

5. We all have to choose whether to live out of our own strength and spirit or to live out of the strength of the Holy Spirit. The choice is an obvious one, but why is this so difficult for us to practice?

6. What will you do this week to live out of God's Holy Spirit?

NINE
IT'S MISSIONAL

We are products of our past,
but we don't have to be prisoners of it.
—Rick Warren[9]

He was twenty-three years old when it happened. After a night of heavy drinking and partying, Justin Maslanka was driving home. Not only was he driving while drunk, he was moving at a very high rate of speed. The car careened out of control, bounced across the road, and came to a halt when it hit a large tree.

To say the car was totaled is an understatement. The bumper was mangled, the entire frame twisted, and every window shattered. But somehow, Justin survived the crash. The car bent in a shape that allowed just enough space for his head and body to survive. It was a miracle, and he knew it.

While Justin was recovering from his injuries, his mom provided the needed statement to accompany this dose of reality: "God saved your life, Justin! You should be dead right now. I have been praying for you all along, and I believe that God has spared you for a purpose. It's time you get right with God."

It's not that Justin didn't know the truth about Jesus. He had been to church. He'd attended the youth ministry at Allison Park Church off and on. He believed there is a God. He understood who Jesus is and that He died on the cross for us. He had no issue with the concept of God or His purpose for us. He just didn't feel the need to surrender his life to Jesus. He described his attitude with these words: "Maybe later, when I'm older and I've had my fun, then I'll surrender my life to God."

But after that near-death experience, Justin was ready to get his life right with God. The very next day, he gave his life to Jesus Christ. He started to attend Allison Park Church on a regular basis, but he knew that he needed to do more, so he got involved in the youth ministry. This gave him an opportunity to be mentored by Cullen Allen, who was serving as the youth pastor at the time.

Cullen told Justin about the baptism in the Holy Spirit. He sat down with him and explained what Jesus had said to His disciples in Acts 1:8: "*You will receive power when the Holy Spirit comes upon you; and you will be my witnesses in Jerusalem, and in all Judea and Samaria, and to the ends of the earth.*"

Cullen explained that the Holy Spirit came to give us power for life: "It's not that we get the Holy Spirit at the moment we are baptized in the Holy Spirit; we get the Holy Spirit when we get saved. When we are baptized in the Holy Spirit, the Holy Spirit gets us!"

So Cullen prayed for Justin to be baptized in the Holy Spirit. The Spirit of God came upon Justin in a powerful way. Not only could he sense the presence of God, but Justin began to pray aloud in tongues. It was like an explosion of praise coming out of his lips as he threw his head back and was swept away in the flow of God's power. I saw Justin just a few days after this experience.

"Pastor Jeff," he said excitedly, "you won't believe what has happened to me! On Tuesday, I was baptized in the Holy Spirit, and since then, I have already led two people to Christ. Today, I was just hanging out at Borders Bookstore, getting a cup of coffee, and all of a sudden, I felt this urging on the inside that I needed to go over and tell this guy sitting at the table next to me about Jesus. So I told him my story, about how God saved my life in the car crash, and I told him how I surrendered my life to Jesus. He said that was what he needed to do, as well. So I prayed for him right there in Borders!"

Can you see this change?

One moment, Justin was partying, drinking, and running from God. Then God intervened and protected him from death in a horrific collision. So Justin surrendered his life to Jesus, which was what he needed to do to become right with God. He started living for God. He wanted God to use him. Then, after he was baptized in the Holy Spirit, Justin stepped into a dimension of purpose that energized his every moment. He knew he was alive for a purpose, and his purpose was to lead people to be saved through Jesus Christ, in the same way that Jesus had saved him.

Today, Justin Maslanka serves as the pastor of the CityReach Church in Cleveland, Ohio. His church has a Men's Hope Home and is being used powerfully to help addicts and alcoholics get free from life-controlling substances and find hope in a relationship with Christ. Justin is a powerful preacher and is being used all over northern Ohio to lead people to Christ. He would tell you that this capacity to win people to Christ started with his experience of what the Bible calls the baptism in the Holy Spirit.

Let's examine what Jesus promised:

You will receive power when the Holy Spirit comes upon you and you will be my witnesses in Jerusalem, and in all Judea and Samaria, and to the ends of the earth.   (Acts 1:8)

Remember that Jesus had given His disciples the Great Commission—a charge to go into all the world and make disciples of everyone everywhere and teach them to obey the way that Jesus had taught them to live. This was the purpose Jesus gave to His disciples at that moment, and it is still His purpose for every one of His followers today. He instructed His disciples to wait in Jerusalem for the *gift* that His Father had promised (Acts 1:4).

THE GIFT THAT BRINGS POWER

Jesus said that the gift He was giving—the baptism in the Holy Spirit—would bring power. The word in the Greek that Jesus used is the word *dunamis*, which is a root word from which we get the word "dynamite." It implies an explosive release of power that proves the testimony of those witnessing to the resurrection.

*"You will receive **power** when the Holy Spirit comes upon you and you will be my **witnesses....**"* (Acts 1:8)

Sometimes we forget the context of these statements. What were the disciples to be witnesses of? What had they seen and heard? If someone put them on the stand in a courtroom, what would they testify that they had experienced? These disciples had seen and heard something that had the capacity to change the world!

They had been witnesses to the resurrection of Jesus!

Yes, they had walked with Him during His three years of ministry on earth. Yes, they had watched Him being put on trial, where He was falsely accused, then beaten and crucified. But what was extremely remarkable was the fact that they had seen Jesus alive *after* He had been in the grave for three days! *"After his suffering, he [Jesus] presented himself to them and gave many convincing proofs that he was alive"* (Acts 1:3).

Jesus is alive, and He wants to prove it to the world! He is looking for people who will represent Him on earth and work with Him to prove it to those who need someone to testify to them about His resurrection and His ongoing activity on earth today. The Holy Spirit was imparted to the disciples to give them power to prove the reality of the resurrection.

Simon Peter provided proof of the resurrection in Acts 3. He released physical healing to a crippled beggar at the temple, and the man began walking and jumping and declaring the healing power of a risen Jesus. He said:

> *Fellow Israelites why does this surprise you? Why do you stare at us as if by our own power or godliness we had made this man walk? The God of Abraham, Isaac and Jacob, the God of our fathers, has glorified his servant Jesus. You handed him over to be killed.... You killed the author of life, but God raised Him from the dead. We are witnesses of this.*
>
> (Acts 3:12–13, 15)

The baptism in the Holy Spirit allowed Peter to step into the power of God in such a way as to see miracles released in the world. The baptism in the Holy Spirit was the gateway to the supernatural in Peter's life, and it can be the gateway to the supernatural release of God's power in your life.

In 2006, I had the opportunity to be part of a huge outreach (we call them festivals) in Harar, Ethiopia. Harar is one of the holiest cities in all Islam: its population is 98 percent Muslim. We went to declare to the people of Harar that Jesus is the Son of God. We went to share the love of God with these Muslims and to offer them proof that Jesus is risen from the dead.

But you can't really prove the resurrection with just words.

There was a man in the city of Harar who was born both deaf and mute. He was forty-two years old. He was well-known in the city because he pumped gas at one of the local gas stations in a prominent place in the city. This man attended the second night of the outdoor festival. One of our team members prayed over him in the name of Jesus, and as he was prayed for, Jesus demonstrated Himself to that city. The man's ears opened up, and he could hear. We brought him up onto the stage and asked him to prove his healing by repeating what he heard. Into the microphone, this man did his best to repeat the syllables that he was now hearing for the very first time.

As you can imagine, this was an incredibly impressive moment. The people in the crowd began to whisper to one another in disbelief, and then they began to laugh, and shout, and dance. Muslims were dancing in the streets at the healing of a deaf man who was cured by being prayed over in the *name of Jesus!* The next night, 17,000 Muslims stood in the field to hear the message of the risen Jesus. Thousands of them prayed to give their lives to Christ.

THE GIFT THAT BRINGS PASSION

You will receive power when the Holy Spirit comes on you; and you will be my witnesses in Jerusalem, and in all Judea and Samaria, and to the ends of the earth.   (Act 1:8)

As soon as Justin Maslanka received the baptism in the Holy Spirit, he had a burden and desire to tell people about Jesus. He carried a burning sensation in his chest. The Holy Spirit was activated within him, and he saw people through the passion of a loving God who wants everyone to be rescued. No one had to tell Justin to share his story with people, and no one had to build him a program to teach him how. The Holy Spirit prompted Justin everywhere he went, and he felt compelled to share.

After I was baptized in the Holy Spirit, I also had an undeniable passion to see my friends come to know Jesus. I was a sophomore in a public high school and had many good friends who didn't have a relationship with Jesus. Every day on my way to school, I felt a burning inside of me compelling me to do something to reach my friends at school. A few of us students got together and started a prayer meeting before the homeroom bell rang to start the day. Slowly, that early morning prayer meeting grew until there were eighty students standing in a circle and praying together in the name of Jesus.

When you're baptized in the Holy Spirit, you'll become part of God's strategic plan to reach the world with the hope of Jesus Christ.

The words of Jesus in Acts 1:8 are strategic. The disciples were to start in Jerusalem, the place where they all lived. It was their hometown, their culture, their comfort zone. But they weren't to stop there. Jesus instructed them to go beyond their comfort zone into all of Judea and Samaria, different locations inhabited by different racial groups and cultures. He wanted them to love beyond their comfort zone and to reach past themselves into places they would never have chosen to go on their own.

As we know, many of these disciples didn't stop with Samaria. They traveled to Europe, India, Africa, China, and beyond. They were driven by a sense of passion for something beyond themselves. No longer were they simply surviving or living boring, passionless lives. They were set on fire to do something with their lives that would last for all eternity.

THE GIFT THAT BRINGS PRODUCTIVITY

The 120 people who gathered in the upper room on the day of Pentecost when the Holy Spirit was first poured out went on to change the world! Think about it, 120 people. Jesus had ministered for three years and had done countless miracles. He had appeared in resurrected form to over 500 people. But only 120 were present in the upper room. Have you ever wondered where all the others were? Three hundred and eighty people saw Jesus after the resurrection, physically alive, and they weren't present to wait for the baptism in the Holy Spirit.

Where were the 5,000 who were fed the loaves and the fishes? Where were the multitudes who had cheered Jesus on Palm Sunday? Where were all those who had been healed or touched in some way? There were only 120 people in the upper room, but after being baptized in the Holy Spirit, those 120 were so empowered they started a revolution that has changed the history of the world.

Today there are two billion people who call themselves Christians. Millions upon millions have been impacted by the gospel over the centuries. Thousands upon thousands became a part of the church in the early stages of its history—all because 120 people were filled with the Holy Spirit and empowered as witnesses of the resurrection of Jesus Christ. We have to admit that it's possible to live out your life as a Christian and yet live an unproductive spiritual life. Some believers live for years and years and...

+ Never personally lead anyone to faith in Christ.

+ Never see anything supernatural happen in answer to their prayers.

+ Never experience freedom from lingering habits and addictive patterns.

+ Never sense the explosive release of the Holy Spirit's passion for the broken.

+ Never feel the rush of the peace, joy, and strength that comes from His presence.

God's purpose for you involves so much more than just your own salvation. He wants you to be part of a revolution to take over the world, not politically or economically but spiritually. He wants to rescue those trapped by sin and selfishness. He wants to protect people like Justin from certain death. He wants to heal and restore and reconnect people to a God who loves them. He wants to offer the world *proof* that He is alive through you.

The adventure of following a living Jesus in what He is doing on planet earth today is waiting for you. This is the opportunity to be infused with, overwhelmed by, and baptized in the Holy Spirit. The chance to see lives changed and miracles released into the world is waiting for you. Would you like to say that you...

+ Personally led hundreds of people to faith in Christ?

+ Prayed and saw the power of God released to heal someone who was sick?

+ Experienced freedom from habits and addictions that held you in the past?

+ Have known the explosive release of the Holy Spirit's joy and power in your life as you have worshipped Him?

Are you hungry for something more? Are you ready to be baptized in the Holy Spirit?

CHAPTER NINE DISCUSSION QUESTIONS

1. Where do you feel closest to God and the most in awe of His creation? What feelings do you have when you are there?

2. Have you ever experienced a significant answer to prayer in your life that you would consider a miracle?

3. When God demonstrates His power in the world, what does that prove to people?

4. The Holy Spirit births in us passion for needs or people we previously may have cared little about. What burden has God birthed in your heart through the work of the Holy Spirit?

5. In what way could you let the Holy Spirit use you in this upcoming week?

TEN
IT'S MEDICINAL

You have a God who hears you, the power of love behind you,
the Holy Spirit within you, and all of heaven ahead of you.
If you have the Shepherd, you have grace for every sin,
direction for every turn, a candle for every corner, and an
anchor for every storm. You have everything you need.
—Max Lucado[10]

When I was developing a plan for the second edition of this book, I decided to add a chapter about another way that the baptism in the Holy Spirit benefits our lives. The first edition of the book, which was called *Power for Life*, was written prior to the pandemic and the tensions of 2020 while this second edition is being written as we approach the end of 2021.

Somehow, I have the feeling that we might always look back on the world through the lens of pre-pandemic realities and post-pandemic life. For all of us who lived through it, the year of 2020 especially carried with it boatloads of frustration, division, and tension. As the Lead Pastor of a local church, it was especially trying.

+ After twenty-nine years as a pastor, I felt like I had been thrown in the deep end. There was no manual on how to lead a church while on lockdown due to a global pandemic.

+ People were dealing with paralyzing fear of catching the virus and dying.

+ Others were feeling anger at the restrictions being imposed by the government, or at the lack of compliance that some were showing toward the requirements of masks and distancing.

+ Within weeks, people began to leave the church. This was not unique to Allison Park Church. People were leaving almost every church. Either the church was too compliant with the CDC or not compliant enough. Some were mad about the leadership's response, but many were also confused and offended that the people they had been worshipping next to for years didn't share their same concerns in this unprecedented time.

+ This meant the loss of friends that I had pastored for years. All of a sudden, in some people's minds, I was a "false prophet" or a "sheep," being led around by the whim of every government official. The words stung. The insults stuck. I realize that it wasn't really me that they were mad at, but the larger situation at hand. But there is no getting around the fact that it still hurt like crazy when they left.

+ Then came the death of Ahmad Arbery, George Floyd, and others. Racial tensions. Riots in the streets. Pressure to speak up. Pressure not to speak up too much. Pressure to use the proper phrases and to avoid association with radical groups.

+ Added to all of that was the fact that it was an election year and the tensions between pro-Trump and anti-Trump members was constant.

The pandemic affected many lives with physical sickness and death and also burdened those left behind with the age-old spiritual questions of why some people suffer and die and others are healed. But more than that, I saw that the pandemic was affecting my congregation, the people around me, and my own spirit with a disease of the soul that was just as dangerous and debilitating, and if we did not recognize and respond to it, there was a potential to lose so much more.

Around July of 2020, I realized a few things:

First, social media and the news are not healthy for my spirit! I started to tune out the constant stream of information and opinion.

Second, there is no way to keep everybody happy. No matter what decision I made, I would please one group and offend another.

But third, I needed healing emotionally from the stress, grief, and pain that I was carrying around with me every day. I was confused. The situations and recommended restrictions were changing every day. I felt like I was in over my head. Overwhelmed. Alone. That's when I remembered the verses that we have already studied in chapter 4 of this book. Listen to the words of Romans 8:26–27 in the *Passion Translation*:

> *And in a similar way, the Holy Spirit takes hold of us in our human frailty to empower us in our weakness. For example, at times we don't even know how to pray, or know the best things to ask for. But the Holy Spirit rises up within us to super-intercede on our behalf, pleading to God with emotional sighs too deep for words.*

In my confusion, grief, and pain, I started to pray in the Spirit. In fact, the choice to pray out in my spiritual language and groan out to God became an inner reflex every time I felt the weight of stress upon my chest. This expression of deep sighs to

God gradually became the only practical way for me to navigate through my day.

When I would feel these overwhelming negative emotions inside, I would find a private place alone with God and just begin to let the Holy Spirit groan out my prayers to heaven. It felt like the Spirit was lifting a pile of rubble off my chest one brick at a time. It was like the Spirit started to let in a little ray of sunlight into the darkened place of my inner soul. It was like walking into an air-conditioned room when you have been working out in the heat of a humid, ninety-degree summer day.

After practicing this pattern for a few days, I started to realize something. God was healing me!

When I was a kid, I used to play with Nerf basketballs and footballs. Nerf balls can be squeezed and mashed, but when the pressure is released, they come back into full form and function. It was like the pandemic of 2020 had squeezed my soul into a tiny little wad of nothing. But when I prayed in the Spirit, my soul was restored. It bounced back and returned to form.

PRAYING IN THE SPIRIT IS AN OUTLET

As human beings, we were not built to carry around the stress that comes with inner turbulence. Wounds from broken relationships. Grief from unexpected loss. Stress from unrealized dreams. Frustration from the expectations of others. Hurt and hopelessness from life's disappointments and pain.

The psalmist David writes in Psalm 55:17, *"Evening, morning and noon I cry out in distress, and he hears my voice."*

What a powerful practice it is to cry out to God when we feel inner distress. The Hebrew words used in Psalm 55 that are translated *"cry out"* indicate the idea of "making noise, to murmur, to growl, or groan as a way to express concern and even complaint."

Can you see the parallel to the verses in Romans 8, *"pleading to God with emotional sighs too deep for words"*?

Even Jesus had a moment where He was at a loss for words and could only sigh, which is recorded for us in Mark 7. Jesus encountered a man who was deaf. The man's condition was so heavy on Jesus's heart that in the process of bringing healing to the man, He let out a deep sigh.

> [Jesus] *took him aside, away from the crowd, Jesus put his fingers into the man's ears. Then he spit and touched the man's tongue. He looked up to heaven and **with a deep sigh** said to him, "Ephphatha!" (which means "Be opened!"). At this, the man's ears were opened, his tongue was loosened and he began to speak plainly.* (Mark 7:33–35)

This type of sigh is like the pressure building up in a tea kettle. As the water begins to boil, the steam has to escape somehow. When it bursts out of the opening at the top of the kettle, the steam explodes with sound. It's almost like you can feel the relief from the pressure building up inside.

When we cry out, sigh deeply, and groan in prayer, it releases the pressure inside. Not only does God hear but He answer our wordless prayers. The vocalization of our prayers is like the release of a pressure valve which begins the process of healing within our soul.

PRAYING IN THE SPIRIT IS AN INFUSION

Now, if all that Holy Spirit birthed groaning did for us was provide a cathartic pressure valve release, I guess that would be one level of value added to our lives. But this practice not only lets something out that needs a release, but it also invites something to be imparted within us.

Consider again the words of Jesus in John 7:37–39:

"Let anyone who is thirsty come to me and drink. Whoever believes in me, as Scripture has said, rivers of living water will flow from within them." By this he meant the Spirit, whom those who believed in him were later to receive. Up to that time the Spirit had not been given, since Jesus had not yet been glorified.

What a description! It's like a geyser that explodes from beneath the surface of the earth. It not only quenches your inner thirst, but it also provides an explosive flow of life within you at the same time. Praying in the Spirit is an activation of that flow of life. It's like shaking a bottle of Mountain Dew. You can see that there is an activation of something on the inside that will explode out of the container whenever the cap is released.

Consider what we are talking about right now. Or maybe I should say consider *Who* we are talking about right now. The Holy Spirit gets activated within you when you groan out, cry out, and pray out in the Spirit. However, what is released is not a thirst-quenching liquid like water. It's a force or power that provides inner strength to your soul.

We are talking about the Spirit of God! The same Spirit hovered over the waters during the creation of the universe (Genesis 1). The same Spirit was involved in bringing the dead body of Jesus back to life (Romans 8). The third person of the Godhead is now exploding onto the scene into your wounded, grieving, exhausted soul.

Paul describes the effect of this relationship in 1 Corinthians 14:4–5, *"Anyone who speaks in a tongue edifies themselves, but the one who prophesies edifies the church. I would like every one of you to speak in tongues."*

When we pray in the Spirit, we are involved in a self-edifying activity. The word *edify* means "to build up, to add strength, to provide consistency and courage to your inner being" according to *The Dictionary of Biblical Language*. What you were lacking before has now been strengthened and fortified through the Spirit. Jude describes something similar in the New Testament:

> *But you, dear friends, by building yourselves up in your most holy faith and praying in the Holy Spirit, keep yourselves in God's love as you wait for the mercy of our Lord Jesus Christ to bring you to eternal life.* (Jude 20–21)

The phrases used in the Greek here to say "*building yourselves up*" imply that you are making the foundation of your confidence, assurance, and conviction in Christ strong by praying in the Spirit, which adds layer upon layer, or brick upon brick, into the establishment of your faith.

PRAYING IN THE SPIRIT IS A COOPERATION

Healing comes to our soul because of two key factors. It's what we let out of our soul when we are in pain. It's a release over inner pressure and stress. Also, it's about what we allow into our soul when we are in need. The Holy Spirit floods into those places of pain and brings strength, healing, and peace.

But in the process of cooperating and operating with the person of the Holy Spirit, our expressions of deep sighs and groans are actually translated into prayer. The Spirit carries our painful cries to God and conveys not just what we feel, but what we need. Isn't that amazing to you? I know it is to me!

> The Spirit helps us in our weakness! We don't know what we should pray for, but the Holy Spirit (who is our most intimate friend and companion) is able to pray through us, and translate what we need even as we groan out in prayer.

And when He prays, His prayers always hit the target. He asks for things that God wills to give us. So the prayers are as accurate and effective as they ever could possibly be. (My paraphrase of Romans 8:26–27)

The healing that flows into our soul is not just due to a cathartic moment where I let out my pain and let in His peace. Part of the healing is in knowing that heaven is hearing and is releasing into my life and my situations the exact right thing that is needed at the moment.

What an awesome, incredible partnership we have with the Holy Spirit!

Your experience with the baptism in the Holy Spirit, and your choice to continue to activate those gifts in your life, prepares you to face the most painful and challenging moments of your life. Practicing God's presence as you pray out in tongues is training for the prayers you will need to pray when you have no idea how you are going to survive. It's preparation for the worst moments of life because you are learning to partner with the most effective partner you could ever have, the person of the Holy Spirit.

PRAYING IN THE SPIRIT IS A RESTORATION

Finally, the result of these aspects of the Holy Spirit's healing and strengthening partnership is that your soul comes back to full health and wholeness. It's like the psalmist David wrote in his most famous song (Psalm 23). *"He makes me lie down in green pasture; He leads me beside quiet waters. He restores my soul"* (verses 1–3 NASB).

A few years ago, I traveled down to the nation of Nicaragua to serve in ministry to pastors and leaders who are part of the Hosanna Church there in Managua. It was blazing hot. I was outfitted in my suit, tie, and jacket. Every day, I spoke for several sessions. Following each session, I would take time to pray for those who needed ministry. It was exhilarating and exhausting all at the same time.

I did not realize at the time that I was not drinking enough liquid. My body was sweating profusely, but I was not replenishing enough. When I flew back to Pittsburgh, I became deathly ill. I was feverish, chilled, and shaking. Nothing I drank or ate seemed to help. The medicine I was taking didn't even seem to touch my symptoms.

When I arrived in the Emergency Room, they diagnosed my condition as dehydration. Immediately, they hooked me up to an IV. I laid there for several hours and slept while my system was infused with the liquid that I needed. When the process was completed, it was incredible how quickly I bounced back.

The fever was gone. The chills disappeared. My energy returned to normal. I was no longer dizzy or lightheaded. When I stood on my feet again, it was as if I had never even had the problem at all.

This is the impact of the Holy Spirit's work as well. When He restores our soul, He does excellent work. There is nothing lacking in what He provides.

It's not that the pain of loss is reduced. It may not be that the memory of the betrayal completely disappears. It's not that the complications with the divorce you are walking through are immediately removed from your life and your ex starts treating you right. It's just that your condition is no longer one of severe depletion. When you stand on your feet again, your strength has fully returned. Now you are ready to face the pain, the problem, or the person who is causing you grief. Now you can start to make sense of what has just happened and how you are going to find a pathway forward.

No doubt, one of the most painful moments of my life happened back in 2016. My wife Melodie and I have five amazing children. We have four boys and a girl. But up until 2016, we had never had a grandbaby. My son Josh and his wife Alyson were expecting their first. We knew it was a girl and we were eagerly awaiting the moment when she would be delivered.

I will never forget getting the phone call. Alyson was at the hospital in labor, but something was wrong. The doctors could no longer hear the baby's heartbeat. They were gravely concerned and had admitted Alyson into a specialized care room.

We raced to the hospital, praying the entire way, and hoping for the situation to resolve. When we arrived, we met our son Josh in the hallway. He informed us that baby Norah had been delivered, but when she came out she was no longer alive. We hugged him and sobbed. He then led us into the room where Alyson was, with her mom, and where baby Norah lay in the little delivery crib.

She was wrapped up nice and tight like any other newborn baby. It was such a strange emotion to see her lying there and yet to know that she was already gone. Probably the most surreal moment I have ever experienced was standing in that delivery room, watching my own little boy, Josh, holding his stillborn little girl in his arms.

We joined hands in the room and prayed, just like I have done hundreds of times before in situations where a family in my church has lost a loved one. We committed Norah to God. We confessed in faith that one day we would get to meet her in the next life, even though we never got to meet her in this life. Eventually, they took her away to prepare her body for burial.

There are moments in time when your family is suffering that you feel the need to stay strong so that they can rely on you. I found myself trying to stay focused to care for the details. For instance, I met with the Funeral Director. We arranged the place of burial. We paid for a little marker to visit in the cemetery where she was buried.

We arranged a brief family-only memorial service at the cemetery. It was brutal, the worst feelings of grief and loss that I have ever personally endured. At first, I was not really processing it all very well. I was just getting up every morning and forcing myself to walk through the day in a daze.

During that time, my wife and I were also training to run a half marathon. I took a few days off from my training for all of these family events. Then, I chose to go out for a long run. I am not sure exactly how the physical expression of energy unlocked my soul, but about a mile into the run, I started to sob. I walked off the trail and laid flat on my back in the grass while tears poured down my face, and groans extended from my chest.

It was a breaking point for me. I guess you could say that was when the pressure valve of my soul unlocked, and all the steam of my grief escaped. That day was the first day in a series of weeks where I was able to groan out my grief to God. My wife and I took a few days off and got away. We talked together. We took some long walks just to let it all sink in that what had happened was actually real.

A major part of the recovery process was the ability to pray out in the Spirit. My groans of grief were turned into expressions of prayer, and I stepped out in faith and prayed in tongues. Again, my mind did not know how to pray or even what to say to God. But the Holy Spirit knew. He helped me connect with the Father. He infused me with his life and peace. He carried my burden for my Josh and Alyson to heaven.

What I won't say to you is that somehow this removed the pain or made everything seem perfect again. That's impossible when you have suffered a great loss. What I will tell you is that praying in the groans of the Spirit helped my soul to be restored.

JESUS HAS OVERCOME THE WORLD

There are so many moments in life where we are hurt, betrayed, grieving, and wounded by people and events that are out of our control. Jesus even said, *"In this world you will have trouble"* (John 16:33). Other versions translate it as "tribulation." No one is exempt from that. Followers of Jesus have trouble. People of faith suffer loss. Those who attempt good things in the world are betrayed. It's just part of the journey here on earth.

Here's the full statement from Jesus, *"I have told you these things, so that in me you may have peace. In this world you will have trouble. But take heart! I have overcome the world"* (John 16:33).

Three things are promised in these sentences.

1.   You will have trouble.

2.   You will have peace.

3.   You will overcome the world, because Jesus has already done that for us.

It's the Holy Spirit's delight to be able to lead you into that overcoming peace. It's His job to bring you to the place where you have not only recovered, but you are ready to overcome. Your choice to pray in the Spirit does not remove the trouble, but it does allow and enable the Holy Spirit to do in you what He does best.

The year of 2020 was destructive to many souls and challenged the faith of many Christians. Unable to worship corporately due to restrictions, and challenged by all the events in the world, many were discouraged and disheartened about God's presence or involvement in His church and on this earth that He created.

The solution to enhancing our faith and finding our way as a community of believers is not to argue until we agree or break up into factions to support our position. No, the way to work toward healing for ourselves, our congregations, and the church as a whole is to cry out to God, through the Holy Spirit, for His power to be released into the situation. He knows what we need, He can see the whole picture, and He is waiting to act with the very response we need if we will just invite Him to work through us, as I have been talking about throughout this book.

To quote the ads of 2020, "now more than ever," it is time to make the baptism in the Holy Spirit our "new normal."

CHAPTER TEN DISCUSSION QUESTIONS

1. Describe a time when you were the most physically, emotionally, or personally exhausted.

2. What kinds of activities are replenishing and restorative to you?

3. Has prayer felt like an outlet or release of pressure to you?

4. In what way to you relate to Jesus's response in Mark 7:33–35?

5. When you read Jesus's promise in John 16:33, what does this promise mean to you?

CONCLUSION

Faith is taking the first step,
even when you don't see the whole staircase.
—Dr. Martin Luther King Jr. [11]

One of my favorite memories as a little boy was our holiday visits to Grandma's house. The most poignant moment was walking through the front door and smelling all the pies and cookies she had been baking for us. As I write these words, I can almost smell the apple pie and chocolate chip cookies! It's making me hungry just thinking about it!

That's the same effect I hope this book has had upon you. My desire is to make you hungry for a greater work of the Holy Spirit in your life. I want you to hunger for the impact of a life that is lived full of the Spirit of God.

IF YOU HAVE YET TO EXPERIENCE THE BAPTISM IN THE HOLY SPIRIT

I hope you'll ask Jesus to do what He promised to do in your life. Remember Jesus is the baptizer in the Holy Spirit. John the

Baptist said, *"He will baptize you with the Holy Spirit and fire"* (Matthew 3:11).

He wants to fill you to overflowing with the Holy Spirit. He wants to saturate your life with the power and presence of God, like a sponge dipped in a bucket of water. Ask Jesus to do what He promised. Can you imagine it?

+ Peace will flood every cell in your being.

+ Joy will erupt from the depths of who you are.

+ Like an electrical current flows through a wire to power an appliance, the Holy Spirit will flood through your being to empower your life.

You may ask, is this really for me? Hear the word of the apostle Peter on the Day of Pentecost. *"You will receive the gift of the Holy Spirit. The promise is for you and your children and for all who are far off—for all whom the Lord our God will call"* (Acts 2:38–39).

Can it be any clearer? *This promise is for you!* Let me recommend some practical steps:

+ Set aside time for prayer and worship in a place where you can be alone and sing and pray out loud.

+ Invite a friend or a spiritual leader (your pastor) or your small group to pray with you, especially someone who has been baptized with the Holy Spirit.

+ Ask Jesus to baptize you with the Holy Spirit. (You may want to have a pastor or leader pray over you at this point and have them ask Jesus to fill you with the Holy Spirit.)

+ Verbalize your worship and prayers loud enough for you to hear yourself. Remember that the gateway to the release of God's power in your life is your lips.

+ Try to speak in tongues. Yes, you read that right. God will not speak in tongues for you. It is a step of faith that you must take. So try.

I got hung up on that last step. My thought was that if it was going to happen, it would need to be much more dramatic than that. It would need to be an almost uncontrollable impulse. I would hardly be able to contain myself. It would not be me at all; it would be all God.

But remember that speaking in tongues is the first step in your new partnership with the Holy Spirit. God wants to do other supernatural things through you as well. Your willingness to step out in faith and act or speak is the way all the other miracles will happen in your life.

You need to tune in to the Holy Spirit as you worship. When you sense or hear in your spirit any small syllables, just speak out what you hear. Remember that when a small child speaks their first words, they don't speak in full sentences. They speak just some simple words and phrases. Their speech isn't perfect. It doesn't have to be. It's a beginning and that's all that matters.

The same is true when you speak in tongues. It doesn't have to be perfect. No dad or mom says to a child, "No. That's not correct! It's not Dada; it's Daddy. Say it again!" When the child says "Dada," everyone goes crazy with joy because the child is beginning to talk. Your heavenly Father feels the same way about you.

You won't understand it. You won't be perfect at it. But that isn't really the point anyway. What's important is that the Holy Spirit is being released through you. He is praying through you. You are beginning to partner with Him to do something beyond the natural. As you step out in faith, Jesus fills you with the Holy Spirit.

Honestly, I can't wait for you to experience this! And when you do, I have provided a place to contact me at the end of this book. I would love to hear your story. Tell me what happens in your life as you ask Jesus to baptize you in the Holy Spirit.

MAYBE YOU HAVE BEEN BAPTIZED IN THE HOLY SPIRIT AT SOME POINT IN YOUR LIFE, BUT YOU HAVEN'T STAYED ACTIVE IN YOUR PARTNERSHIP WITH THE HOLY SPIRIT.

Remember that the baptism in the Holy Spirit isn't designed to be an event you seek, experience, and then move on from. It's designed to be a gateway into an entirely new way of life. It's about providing proof of the resurrection. It's about accessing the disposition, capacity, and companionship of the Holy Spirit. It's about being used of God to provide divine solutions for people in need.

You have to activate this process in your life:

+ Spend time daily in worship. Psalm 22 tells us that God inhabits or is enthroned upon the praises of His people. Invite Him to come and rest upon your life as you worship.

+ Pray in the Spirit and speak in tongues every day. This is what Paul said about his own life, *"I thank God that I speak in tongues more than all of you"* (1 Corinthians 14:18). He understood the impact this practice had on his spiritual life. Paul was transformed in his character, edified in his soul, empowered to do supernatural things, and strengthened in his effectiveness in prayer.

+ Begin to believe that God wants to use you in a mighty way. Don't just live to survive your life, live to make a difference. Live to be used of God.

FINALLY, IF YOU ARE ACTIVE IN ALL OF THIS, I HOPE THIS BOOK HAS INSPIRED YOU TO BELIEVE FOR EVEN MORE THAN EVER BEFORE.

You might want to become even more intentional in your walk with God. I would encourage you to schedule times where you step out to minister to others and believe God for His miraculous release.

+ Plan to go on a mission trip.

+ Join a street ministry team.

+ Ask your pastor if you can join the prayer teams that lay hands on the sick at your church.

+ Visit hospitals and pray for someone in need.

+ Look for opportunities to be used at work, school, or in your neighborhood.

God wants to do so much more in your life than what you have experienced. Since the Holy Spirit is God, He can do anything God can do. And since the Holy Spirit lives within you, He can do whatever God can do through your life. You become an active partner with Almighty God to see His power released on earth.

Again, I would love to hear from you as you take this journey forward with the Holy Spirit. May God use you to change the world, one life at a time by the power of His Spirit in your life.

ENDNOTES

1. Mark Batterson, *Wild Goose Chase: Reclaim the Adventure of Pursuing God* (Colorado Springs, CO: Multnomah Books, 2008), 4.

2. Francis Chan, *Forgotten God: Reversing Our Tragic Neglect of the Holy Spirit* (Colorado Springs: David C. Cook, 2009), 37.

3. Jack Hayford Quotes – http://www.azquotes.com/quote/1395306.

4. George Stormont, *Smith Wigglesworth,: A Man Who Walked with God* (Tulsa, OK: Harrison House, 2010), 39.

5. Erin, "How Well Do Dogs Hear?" PetMeds Spotlight, February 2, 2013, https://www.petmeds.org/petmeds-spotlight/how-well-do-dogs-hear/.

6. Andrew Murray, *Absolute Surrender* (West Conshohocken, PA: Infinity, 2014), 35.

7. Bruce Wilkinson, *You Were Born for This: 7 Keys to a Life of Predictable Miracles* (Colorado Springs: Waterbrook Multnomah, 2011), 46.

8. Chris Hodges, *Fresh Air: Trading Stale Spiritual Obligation for a Life-Altering, Energizing, Experience-It-Everyday Relationship*

with God (Carol Stream, IL: Tyndale Momentum, 2012), 192.

9. Rick Warren, *The Purpose Driven Life: What on Earth Am I Here For?* (Grand Rapids, MI: Zondervan, 2002), 28.

10. Max Lucado. *Traveling Light: Premier Library Edition* (Nashville, TN: Thomas Nelson Inc., 2009), 33.

11. Martin Luther King Jr., https://www.brainyquote.com/ quotes/ quotes/m/martinluth105087.html?src=t_step.

ABOUT THE AUTHOR

Jeff Leake is a pastor, author, speaker, church planting expert, and apostolic leader with a heart to build the kingdom. He has served as Lead Pastor of Allison Park Church in Pittsburgh, Pennsylvania, for more than thirty years. During that time, Allison Park Church has tripled in size while parenting thirty-one new churches and launching seven additional campuses.

Jeff's insights on Spirit-led leadership, church health and growth, and church multiplication have helped leaders, pastors, and churches across the Northeastern United States to grow and flourish. Jeff is one of the founding Lead Team members of the Church Multiplication Network, the Founder and President of the Allison Park Leadership Network, and the Executive Director of the Network of Hope, a nonprofit group that meets people's spiritual and practical needs. He is also the author of several books, including *Praying with Confidence: Thirty-One Days of Powerful Moments with God, God in Motion: Making Sense of the Loose Ends in Life,* and *Twelve Trends in Multiplication: A Study in Reproducing Churches.*

Jeff has a bachelor's degree in Bible from Evangel University and a master's degree in missiology from the Assemblies of God Theological Seminary. He and his wife, Melodie, have been married for over thirty-five years and have five children and six grandchildren.

FOR MORE INFORMATION

For more information about this and other valuable resources, or to share your story with the author, visit:

AllisonParkLeadershipNetwork.com/
GatewaytotheSupernatural

Additional resources for church leaders are available at allisonparkleadershipnetwork.com.

Welcome to Our House!

We Have a Special Gift for You

It is our privilege and pleasure to share in your love of Christian books. We are committed to bringing you authors and books that feed, challenge, and enrich your faith.

To show our appreciation, we invite you to sign up to receive a specially selected **Reader Appreciation Gift**, with our compliments. Just go to the Web address at the bottom of this page.

God bless you as you seek a deeper walk with Him!

WE HAVE A GIFT FOR YOU. VISIT:

whpub.me/nonfictionthx

WHITAKER
HOUSE